'Tainted Blood'

AP Wolf

Published in 2020 by FeedARead.com Publishing

A CIP catalogue record for this title is available from the
British Library.

1972.

It was a brave new world, but also a very dangerous one, for if you were not careful as you unlocked and opened the heavy metal gate your hand could easily stick to the frozen metal surface as if it had been super-glued there by the harsh overnight frost of a Hampshire winter. Then, once you had negotiated that hazard and successfully opened the gate, the realisation would suddenly wash over you that what you were about to do was rather stupid, perhaps suicidal and that it could be described politely as 'foolhardy', or perhaps impolitely as 'sheer bloody insanity'. For you were about to open a door to allow the most exquisitely dangerous animal in the world to share with you a narrow and confined space, where death or serious injury was a very real possibility, as this immense creature had killed more zoo keepers than any other confined animal, including such overwhelmingly powerful and predatory creatures as lions, tigers, leopards and jaguars.

So, as you opened the door, you instinctively obscured your diminutive human body behind it, so that the gargantuan beast that came hurtling out in a sudden and now unrestrained explosion of frantic energy, would at first ignore you. As he snorted clouds of vapour through his nostrils, flared with excitement, and then stamped his hooves on the hard concrete surface in majestic confrontation, he was wreathed in the ethereal steam of sudden transition from the warmth of his body inside the overnight cell to a freezing Hampshire dawn, that enveloped all in its path with its harsh and unrelenting crystalline frost.

There suddenly, in front of you, was the raw, undiluted essence of East-Africa, as if that stunning stallion had galloped directly from the barren Ethiopian plains and Kenyan bushlands to charge magically into this bizarre landscape of the Hampshire downs.

As you hid behind that fragile door, acutely aware that, with just one powerful kick from his hind legs, this immense and formidable animal could shatter that barrier into a thousand splinters, he capered royally in front of you, arching his short but powerful neck with its Mohawk mane, raising his immense, regal head in warning, as he fixed you firmly with the penetrating gaze of his obvious dominance. He lifted his hooves in a distinctive high-stepping gait, much like a war-horse, as he trotted menacingly up and down the narrow space, where he knew he was the lord and master. For he was the 'Imperial'. And he knew it. And so did you. This 'Imperial' was the largest living wild equid anywhere on this planet – a planet which inherently belonged to him, not you – well over six magnificent feet on his four magnificent hooves. The Grevy's zebra was thus named firstly as the 'Imperial' because of its magnificent stature and stately presence.

However, as you foolishly opened his door, you were stupidly closing the door on him as a thriving and magnificent wild animal and confining him forever on the concrete hard-standing of our naïve misunderstanding, as a practically barren, semi-domesticated creature with no basic instinct for survival in the wilds of East Africa.

These wilds began to disappear in the 1800s - under a relentless incoming tide of Western settlers who farmed and exploited the lands and their wildlife for their own purposes.

The 'Imperial' was first discovered by the Western world in 1882 and one was presented by Menelik II, the King of Ethiopia, to the President of France, Jules Grévy, as the first living specimen ever seen outside Africa.

You had signed up though, to this captivating dream of breeding endangered animals in order to release them, supposedly, back into the wild, so unless you enclosed that capering Grevy's zebra stallion safely onto his separate hard-standing -   because he was too volatile to mix with the herd in their confined winter quarters - to let the gentle zebra mares familiarize themselves through a protective fence with the 'Imperial' stallion, then this captive breeding programme claiming to replenish the dangerously depleted numbers of wild Grevy's zebra, was going nowhere. However, many years later, when your virginity in such matters had been brutally raped by reality, you finally realised that this had been where it was intended that it should go right from the very first day of that Marwellian mirage and cleverly disguised Chipperfield circus: nowhere. Where the reality of vested commercial interests was camouflaged by the futile claim to be mending the planet and by the ill-conceived, bizarre notion of reintroducing captive-bred animals back into the wild, although that 'wild' was vastly diminished! Which eventually led to … nowhere.

So in the end, all you had at that point in time, was your overwhelming love of the exotic creatures that had come into your personal care. This love would be the only survivor, as behind you would be scattered the tragic road-kill of so many beautiful and endangered wild animals.

This tragedy had its origins in 1820, when Lord Morton valiantly, but vainly, tried to turn back the inexorable tide of extinction by creating the very first 'captive breeding program' in the world, in an attempt to save the severely endangered Quagga. A noble effort in that largely ignoble age, but doomed to the same ultimate failure as the later 'trendy' safari and wildlife park fashion of the 1970's and 1980's which claimed to do the same thing. For Lord Morton's failure was caused by not only the dearth of breeding stock available to him, but also by the almost impossible task, in his era, of transporting live animals from the wilds of East-Africa, across the seas to his estates in England. The good Lord Morton's solution, in his frustration, was to cross breed his one and only Quagga, a stallion, with a horse, resulting in the production of a faintly striped hybrid, this rare event being recorded by the Royal Society in 1820. As we will later see in this volume, such bizarre and ill-fated hybrid zoo animals were to once again become very fashionable in the zoological institutions some 150 years later.

The problem however, for the much later zoos in the 1970s and 1980s involved in the trendy new-age fashion of supposedly reintroducing captive bred stock - of which there was plenty - back into the wild, was that this 'wild' no longer existed. As all their vain and vague efforts had gone into captive breeding programs, they and the rest of the world, silently watched as the natural habitats of East Africa were over-run by human greed, war, and relentless over-grazing by domestic livestock. All compounded by a complete and utter misunderstanding on the part of the people and organisations, concerning the delicate balance of mankind, nature and environment.

So, at least Lord Morton's proposed captive breeding program made sense in 1820 because wild East Africa was still very much there, even if the Quagga wasn't, whereas these trendy later attempts had their 'Quaggas' aplenty but had irretrievably lost wild East Africa. In other words, poor old Lord Morton had only one captive animal but plenty of prime land for their reintroduction into their original habitat, whereas the modern zoos and wildlife parks had, and still have, a truly massive 'surplus' of captive animals but almost no safe habitat to reintroduce them into.

This is a continuing farce taking place even today, which has recently seen one so-called 'conservation' wildlife park in southern England claiming to 'reintroduce' Grevy's zebra back into the 'wild' in an East-African country where Grevy's zebra probably never occurred in the first place: Djibouti.

Three entirely independent and separate specialist researchers avow that there are no confirmed records in history of Grevy's zebra ever occurring in Eritrea and Djibouti!

This much vaunted and highly acclaimed 'reintroduction' back into the 'wild' was composed of three unwanted surplus Grevy's zebra stallions, shipped off thousands of miles, to end up spending the rest of their days munching hay in a small zoo enclosure in a primitive safari park just outside Djibouti city, with no females. Now that is 'extinction'.

Lord Morton would have thoroughly appreciated the irony of that particular farce.

In a similarly farcical manner, these modern zoological proponents and members of the captive breeding programme for Grevy's zebra, attach themselves by proxy in a variety of ways - most often by donating small sums of money - to East African wildlife and environmental agencies, so that the name of their zoological institution is associated with those agencies.

They claim what they term a 'successful reintroduction' of Grevy's zebra to certain areas of the Tsavo National Park in Kenya in 1964 and 1977 when, in two waves, a total of 140 Grevy's zebra were 'successfully reintroduced back into the wild'. This is wishful thinking at best, simply because the majority of these zoological institutions that subsequently attached themselves to this so called 'successful reintroduction back into the wild', were not in existence in 1964. They were certainly not in a position to export captive bred animals anywhere, as they had not been bred in any useful numbers by 1977. In fact the Grevy's zebras concerned here had never been in captivity, so they were not captive bred at all, as they were, in fact, all wild animals that had been 'relocated' by the East African wildlife agencies involved, to Tsavo from Isiolo, because of the grave threats they supposedly faced there from poaching and acute grazing competition from domestic livestock. The salient fact that even these relocated wild Grevy's zebra could not survive the rigours of their new habitat, being reduced in number by 2014 to a mere 26 animals, does not bode well for any 'successful reintroduction' of captive bred animals.

The wild population of Grevy's zebra in East Africa was estimated at some 750,000 animals in 1900, but dramatically fell to a mere 15,000 animals by the late '60s, which is exactly when the zoos and wildlife parks of the world decided that they wanted wild Grevy's Zebra to breed them in captivity, supposedly to save them from extinction in the wild. So they paid Western animal trappers and dealers to capture the animals, mostly foals - severely disrupting the delicate, natural balance of the zebra herds and the environment they inhabited - to scatter them across the world's zoos.

Meanwhile, they ignored the fact that the natural habitat for Grevy's in East Africa was being eroded by domestic livestock while they were removing large proportions of the remaining herds for their far-off zoological collections, leaving behind them a mere 2,000 Grevy's zebra in East Africa by 1977. This was a catastrophic decline in the wild Grevy's herds of almost 80% in those ten few years, while the incidence of wild caught Grevy's zebras in zoological gardens in those years saw an 80% increase.

Go figure! Of course, other contributory factors in this rapid decline in the population of wild Grevy's have played a role in their sudden demise, amongst them being the severe decline of suitable habitat due to the ever-increasing numbers of domestic livestock, and critically in Ethiopia, the careless introduction of invasive foreign vegetation, such as the mesquite plant.

A factor that is widely unrecorded and largely unknown in regard to the alarming collapse of the Grevy's zebra population, from a high of 750,000 in 1900 to a scant population of 15,000 in all of Kenya in the 1970's, is the dreadful aftermath of World War II on the endemic wildlife, particularly zebras, in Kenya and other East African countries.

In 1942 the Kenyan game warden, Noel Simon, on a trip to Kenya, was able to record vast herds of zebra roaming across the plains, easily visible from the train track that cut through the country, but when he returned in 1945, zebras, especially the Grevy's zebra, had all but disappeared from those plains. They were wiped out, he notes, by the efforts of the colonial government of Kenya to feed the tens of thousands of starving Italian prisoners of war who were being held in temporary camps. Just in the Nanyuki districts of 'Selengai' and 'Loita' alone, more than 6,000 zebra were slaughtered in those three years to feed the Italian prisoners, so if one were to apply that number to the rest of Kenya, then the number of zebras slaughtered could have been as many as 20,000 to 30,000 animals, thus explaining the dramatic and sudden decline in the Grevy's zebra population.

This was swiftly followed by a failed attempt to introduce a wheat crop scheme on the Athi plains, which the few remaining Grevy's enjoyed and plundered so much, that the game wardens of the time shot many more thousands of them to preserve the wheat crop, which subsequently failed anyway. This particular farce on the Athi plains, continued into the 1960s with thousands of zebras being shot by the game wardens of the time; their valuable hides being drop-shopped at a mere 15 Kenya shillings a time, just to get rid of them.

This is why the Grevy's zebra became so vulnerable, although once the war was over and the Athi wheat scheme abandoned, those particular pressures would have relented and allowed the remaining wildlife to recover, all other things being equal. However, then the trapping of Grevy's zebra for zoological collections started; between the 1970s and the 1980s, having a massive impact on the surviving pockets of animals. This was when, of course, Marwell Zoo was founded and its Grevy's herd established, with the vast majority of them being wild caught specimens.

One can easily imagine the overwhelming disruption and destruction of the Grevy's herd structure in a wild situation, for even one young foal to be captured alive by determined hunters, driven only by profit. This profit was generated by the comfortable zoo directors sitting in their comfortable armchairs in their very comfortable country mansions in Hampshire and Wiltshire signing the cheques that caused this long-distance mischief, misery and mayhem, which would ultimately lead to the irreversible decline of the Grevy's zebra as a wild animal. Marwell Zoological Park was a prime mover in promoting this relentless and insatiable desire on the part of modern zoos to own and display herds of Grevy's zebra, and in doing so, they very much imperilled the Imperial.

This is the same organisation that now claims to be intimately involved with the 'protection' of Grevy's zebra in the wild.

This was an unnatural and entirely preventable catastrophe, designed and engineered by the very people, and the wildlife organisations they represented, who had been given the crucial task of ensuring that this disaster did not happen. This farce still stands today as a 'conservation' landmark in human greed, ego and seriously misguided ambitions and misdirected funds.

This situation is remarkably illustrated by the fact that at the same time that John Knowles and Marwell Zoo were intimately involved with the live capture of Grevy's zebra in East Africa, then so too was a much honoured and lauded 'Chairman' of the World Wildlife Fund, Tim Walker, close friend of Knowles and a later director of the Marwell Trust. He too, spent lavish sums of money to pay animal dealers for wild caught specimens of rare and endangered ungulates for his private collection of such creatures, at Midway Manor in Wiltshire.

The same species which he was actually empowered, as a very senior member of the World Wildlife Fund, to protect but which he sacrificed to his own altar of ego, in a medieval masquerade of menageries that was nothing but a mirage to disguise the reality of the extinction to which he was actually contributing.

In their vain and inglorious desire to 'own' the last of the species, feeding their private collections, which were nothing but pompous peep shows for the nouveau riche of the age, they were actually wiping them out of existence. For this debacle, these wealthy patrons of the trade in wild caught rare animals were rewarded by Her Majesty the Queen and her government of the day with 'honours' for their role in the 'conservation' of the Grevy's zebra, and other East African ungulates, which were also poised on the brink of extinction.

Chapter Two

So this dream of a 'brave new world' - to which you were fully committed, along with many other young and naïve believers - of the 'captive breeding' of rare and endangered animals being a viable, vital and valuable weapon in the armoury of the conservation and protection of wild animals and their habitats, has actually proven to be, some forty years later, possibly the very worst nightmare. The reality could never match up with the impossible dream of the 1970s zoo's ambitions, in which their much vaunted and somewhat revolutionary 'captive breeding' programs were going to save the endangered animals of the world from extinction. The reality of that impossible dream of a 'brave new world' was badly ruptured and flawed right from the start, simply because, to create the captive herds that were going, supposedly, to save the species from extinction in the wild, the zoos took their breeding stock out of the wild, from the last precarious, scattered herds.

In the particular case of Grevy's zebra in the wilds of East Africa, where the animal's population in the late '60s and early '70s had already seriously declined from other pressures, to almost extinction levels; this was the exact, tragic moment when the somewhat ruthless Western animal dealers, acting on behalf of wealthy zoo owners in England and elsewhere, dealt the fatal blow to the already diminished Grevy's herds by capturing countless numbers of Grevy's foals.

Many of these youngsters died immediately in these violent encounters with the animal catcher's extreme brutality, while many more died in holding camps or in the long transit back to America or Europe.

This perverse concept of the 'captive breeding' of zoo animals as a means of either protecting or nurturing wild animal populations, had, in the case of Grevy's zebra, actually led to wholesale slaughter and the destruction of the Grevy's as a sustainable wild animal, because the trappers had ripped the herds apart, even by shooting protective zebra mares to isolate their foals so that those foals were then easier to catch!

All of this fully sanctioned slaughter and mayhem took place right in front of the national and international agencies responsible for enforcing the strict laws that protected the Grevy's zebra in its East African homeland from the 1970s onwards.

They did absolutely nothing then, just as they still do today, appearing totally incapable of enabling or enforcing any kind of real protective measures to save the Grevy's zebra, instead spending their time and money organising yearly conferences and symposia.

They endlessly discuss what could or might be done to protect the few remaining wild Grevy's herds that are still declining at an alarming rate but they do virtually nothing on the ground, simply producing fancy, expensive reports on what they plan to do in the future. Completely forgetting that the Grevy's zebra has no future, except behind bars.

This woeful and ambivalent attitude towards the extermination of this rare and beautiful 'Imperial' has been the norm now since the late 1960s and early 1970s when the Grevy's herds were virtually smashed into oblivion by the over-whelming demand from the zoos of Europe and America for wild caught foals to form the nucleus of the captive breeding herds of the so-called 'future'.

There can be absolutely no doubt that Marwell Zoo – and its former owner and founder, John Knowles – were complicit in this relentless round-up of the already highly threatened Grevy's zebra wild population, by financing and facilitating the capture of countless Grevy's zebra foals as the raw fuel for their 'brave new world' of captive breeding. With John Knowles portraying himself as the modern 'Noah', and Marwell Zoo as his 'Ark'.

The only problem was, that Knowles' Ark, together with the global 'captive breeding program', was a sinking ship that was taking down rare and vulnerable animals with it. Not two by two, but rather by the hundreds, or even thousands, of stunning 'Imperials'; the Grevy's that either died or were slaughtered as the innocent victims of the warped and twisted vision of Knowles' 'brave new world'. A vision soon shared by a bandwagon of other bastions of the zoo world. It was very much John Knowles who was their early champion, spokesman and the energetic activist in this strange Hampshire field full of exotic East African animals.

The real story has yet to be told of how these wild Grevy's zebras mysteriously arrived at Marwell Zoo from behind the Iron Curtain. At the time, there were no captive breeding herds in the shadowy zoo world, capable of supplying John Knowles with a ready-made herd of Grevy's zebra, so the capture of wild Grevy's foals that formed the very foundation of Marwell Zoo's captive breeding herd today, was the catalyst for the sudden firestorm of extinction that engulfed the 'Imperials'. While John Knowles, the founder and former owner of Marwell Zoo, rushed around the charred remains of that bonfire of the vanities, trying to put that fire out with gasoline. These zoos were very careful indeed to never disclose the carnage that had led to them suddenly becoming the proud owners of some of the rarest ungulates in the world, in numbers which had never before been seen in zoos. This was an unprecedented launch of their 'brave new world' of captive breeding.

John Knowles, in his own published memoirs on Marwell Zoo, refers often to the extraordinary zoological institution located at 'Dvur Kralove' in modern day Czechoslovakia, often remarking what strong and friendly relationships Marwell Zoo and Dvur Kralove enjoyed back in the heady days of the 1970s when 'captive breeding programmes' first emerged. He was a frequent visitor to Dvur Kralove, and many other zoological institutions behind the 'Iron Curtain' of the communist world, normally out of bounds to Western visitors at that time, but he was able to gain entry because of his commercial connections in the newly emerging industry of the factory farming of poultry, in which the communist leaders all had a great interest. So, as the director of Marwell, Knowles was able to exploit these rare opportunities to meet the movers and shakers in that extremely shadowy world of communist exotic animal dealers and their Western agents, like Franz van den Brink and Fred Zeehandelaar. Knowles, and many others, continued these relationships for many years.

Today, Dvur Kralove appears to be a commendable zoological institution, which apparently contributes much to the world of conservation and the preservation of endangered species of animals all over the world. However, the situation at Dvur Kralove has not always been so positive, as back in the late 1960s and early 1970s when Knowles often visited the Czechoslovakian zoo and enjoyed such cordial relationships with the director, Josef Vagner, it was a very different story and a very different 'zoo' indeed.

Josef Vagner became the director of Dvur Kralove in 1965, and for his first three years there, not much changed. Then seemingly out of nowhere, when Soviet tanks invaded and took charge of Czechoslovakia in 1968, he launched the biggest live animal hunt that the world had ever seen.

It seems almost as if he could peer into the near future of the early 1970s and see the massive expansion in American and European safari parks and their ilk, and thus the subsequent demand for wild caught herd animals to fill this sudden rash popping up all over the skin of the planet. He launched expedition after expedition into East Africa, some estimate as many as ten truly massive live animal hunts, between the years of 1968 and 1975. He spent up to eight months of every year there in his relentless pursuit of live animals, where it is estimated that in excess of 3,500 young calves and foals of rare or endangered species of ungulates were captured and transported all the way back to Dvur Kralove.

Leaving behind them a bloody trail of the carcasses of the parents which had obstructed the hunters from capturing the youngsters they needed to fuel the 'captive breeding programmes' of the 'future'. Perhaps that crystal ball was provided by the proponents of the newly launched 'vision' of captive breeding?

Many of the wild-caught East African ungulates with which John Knowles stocked his Marwell Zoo in the early and heady years of the 1970s, came from Dvur Kralove, meaning that the animals carried with them an air of respectability, as they had been exported to Marwell Zoo from Czechoslovakia, not directly from East Africa. Thus the very severe restrictions on the importation into the United Kingdom and export out of East Africa of such rare and endangered animals were somehow overcome by two zoological prestidigitators using a simple bit of 'hey presto'.

Quite remarkable really, but also a tragedy and travesty of immense proportions because the world at large was, and still is, completely unaware of the appalling attrition rates that generally apply to the live capture of wild animals, particularly to ungulate species like the Grevy's, whose protective herding instincts, especially in regard to their foals, make them extremely vulnerable if subjected to such massive expeditions to capture those foals.

Now I, a young, naïve and inexperienced zookeeper at Marwell Zoo in 1973 had the unique privilege of actually touching each one of the Grevy's zebras in the herd there, some even feeding out of my hand, but I had no way of knowing then, just what an awesome privilege that was. Those Grevy's at Marwell Zoo were some of those extremely rare foals that had survived that merciless, never-ending massacre, year after bloody year, by Josef Vagner of Dvur Kralove, aided and abetted by John Knowles and his cronies in other European and American zoos. All expedited by the sinister animal dealers in the background, such as Franz van den Brink and Fred Zeehandelaar.

I didn't know that then, but I know it now. I also now know the absolutely appalling attrition rate of wild caught animals, which tells me that for every Grevy's zebra that I magically touched at Marwell Zoo in 1973, perhaps as many as five to ten other foals and adults died in the wilds of East Africa amidst the mayhem and confusion of John Knowles' vision of a 'brave new world'.

Chapter Three

Mentioned earlier, were the two successful translocations of a large number of wild 'Imperials' from Isiolo in Kenya to Samburu and Tsavo west in 1964 and 1977; with which many zoological institutions appear to associate themselves, many of these captive breeding protagonists claiming it as a successful 'reintroduction' of captive-bred Grevy's into the wilds of East Africa. We know now that these Grevy's were, in fact, wild animals that had been moved, apparently for their own safety, by a private rancher with no affiliation whatsoever to any official conservation body or organisation, but with, however, the consent and agreement of the Kenyan Wildlife Authority. This private individual taking direct action in a somewhat dramatic attempt to save the few remaining Grevy's in Kenya at that time, funded by Hollywood actor William Holden, was the seemingly very knowledgeable rancher Don Hunt. He told reporters at the time that, realising that the local population of Grevy's was in imminent danger of extinction from poaching, domestic livestock incursion and capture for zoos, he undertook the extremely fraught and difficult task of moving the entire sub-population of Grevy's to areas where they might, just might, be able to survive. Carefully capturing the Grevy's one by one using jeeps and nooses, according to him, Don Hunt managed to move the entire herd apparently without a single loss. He said that he realised right from the very start that if he and his team pursued Grevy's relentlessly over a long distance, in the overpowering heat of East Africa, they would risk killing the pursued zebra - especially young foals - from heat exhaustion and shock. So instead of such dangerous and self-defeating tactics - as used at that time by many other live animal trappers, like Josef Vagner and his assorted crew of multi-nationals - Don Hunt described using his jeeps in a team effort, where blocking manoeuvres were cleverly employed to prevent long chases, and in the event of the failure of a short, sharp chase, abandoning the hunt after eight minutes.

As we have just pointed out, Don Hunt's allegedly meticulous approach to the successful capture of live Grevy's zebra was sadly and regrettably not utilised by many of the other live animal trappers of the 60s and 70s. Trappers who instead relied on the brutal and savage techniques that had been in vogue since the early 1900s glory days of Hagenbeck and his carnival of animal trappers, and still practised by Josef Vagner of Dvur Kralove Zoo and his cohorts. Their reckless and relentless tactics of furious pursuit by jeep until the young of the herd had been separated from their protective parents and had collapsed in utter exhaustion, resulted in what has been cheerfully called by zoologists ever since, the "largest shipment of wild-caught animals ever to be seen in the world".

However, what those zoologists probably do realise, but don't tell you, is that this momentous and truly massive shipment of wild-caught animals from East Africa also resulted in the tragic and appalling deaths of thousands of other wild animals - mostly ungulates such as the Grevy's zebra. This is because of the disgraceful and deeply disturbing attrition on animals that died: of exhaustion and shock as a result of the initial chase; during the actual capture; in transit back to the base camp; from poor handling and mismanagement in the base camp; on the extended journey out of Africa and then across Europe to Dvur Kralove and other holding zoos in Europe, or when later transferred to the safari parks and zoos, like Marwell and Longleat.

What the 'International Stud Book for Grevy's Zebra' damningly shows, is that of all the wild-caught Grevy's zebra placed into zoological institutions since records began, 44% of all stallions died before reaching sexual maturity at six years old; and that 25% of all mares died before reaching sexual maturity at three years old. It is certainly obvious that many of these Grevy's zebra did not survive very long once at Dvur Kralove Zoo. Adding to that already alarming attrition rate, one must also consider the remaining wild animals that died, or failed to breed, as a result of the disruption and disintegration of their fragile herd and family structure that these massive game hunts inflicted, and their chaotic impact on the surrounding environment.

These live capture hunts were not just for Grevy's but also for other very rare animals such as the Northern white rhino which was virtually wiped out from parts of its already restricted range in the Sudan by these reckless Western hunters of live animals.

Reports from Peter Litchfield and Annie Olivecrona, co-workers of Vagner and Chipperfield in these East African live animal hunts - do show what a cavalier attitude these Western cowboys of East Africa displayed, with their total disregard for the extremely vulnerable animals they were catching by the thousands at that time. Olivecrona had a long history of working with both men between 1968 and 1975 capturing rare and endangered animals, and is presently described as a 'Swedish conservationist, based in Kenya'. These co-workers of Vagner and Chipperfield describe how spotter planes - usually flown by Vagner and his son - would direct the crews in jeeps on the ground - most often driven by members of the Chipperfield family- to the herds, where a relentless pursuit would take place, continuing until an animal was sufficiently exhausted for

Peter Litchfield, the chief animal catcher, to place a noose around its neck. It would then be transported back to the base camp where Olivecrona, presumably, looked after their needs, having been trained to do so by the Chipperfields, at their safari parks. It was exactly in this manner that the very last calves of the almost extinct Sudanese Northern white rhino were captured, six in total. Five of the calves were then surreptitiously taken out of Sudan and into Uganda by Olivecrona and Chipperfield, from where they commenced the long journey all the way back to Dvur Kralove in the CCSR. Once there, they remained, and slowly faded into extinction anyway; the last remnant dying recently in 2018 with no viable off-spring. Thus, after this wholesale destruction of East African wildlife, Vagner and Chipperfield were proud to call themselves "The world's biggest suppliers of wild animals to zoos and safari parks"

As disgraceful as that situation is, and was, and will always be, it now appears that it could be much, much worse than that, with persistent rumours that some of these animal trappers working at the behest of zoological institutions in Europe and America, actually traded automatic weapons in exchange for wildlife capture and export permits. The same automatic weapons that have played a crucial role in the mass extermination of East Africa's wildlife. If that is the case, then it is some legacy that those private and public zoological institutions have left to the scant wildlife of East Africa.

Chipperfield's main animal catcher, Peter Litchfield, when interviewed many years later about his role as the trapper of the last remaining Sudanese Northern white rhino calves exclaimed: "We put our lives at risk!"

If it is possible to forgive that comment, which it probably isn't, then it might be just as well to remember that these wild-born calves of the Sudanese Northern white rhinos were the last great white hope for their survival as a truly wild species, a hope that was thrashed and dashed by their subsequent transfer to a 'captive breeding programme' at Dvur Kralove Zoo in the CCSR. Forty-three years later, this resulted in their total extinction. A wild animal that had been evolving for millions of years until the hunting and zoo industries claimed them.

This situation can be directly related to the similar demise of the Grevy's zebra, as we watch it unfolding before our very eyes, but, the 'International Stud Book for the Grevy's Zebra' is very up to date at Marwell Zoo, so all is well in their very peculiar world.

Unfortunately in the meantime, in the real 'world', the 'Imperials' have reached their sell-by date in the ever-diminishing wilds of East Africa, thanks to the likes of Chipperfield, Vagner and John Knowles.

Then, to be sure that we know the true nature of the 'beast' we are dealing with here, a comment that Jimmy Chipperfield made in the 1950s after his very first 'safari' to Africa, is rich with the portent of what he, and the other Western animal dealers and traders, intended to visit on the wildlife of East Africa:

"Obviously there was an abundance of animals in that huge country – in fact, I judged that there were far *too* many."

Chapter Four

Returning to what, at first, appear to be the noble efforts of
private rancher, Don Hunt, to rescue the Grevy's zebra in
Kenya from what he called the 'brink of extinction' in the
60s and 70s; all is really not quite as 'noble' as it might
first appear. History has subsequently revealed that Don
Hunt - like many other so-called 'conservationists' who are
also involved in the trade of wild animals - had vast and
vested commercial interests in the Grevy's zebra he
captured in order to move them to 'safer' areas, as many of
those 'safer' areas subsequently proved to be the zoos and
safari parks of Europe and the USA. At the same time that
Don Hunt was translocating them, he was actually fatally
contributing to their collapse as a wild animal in Kenya,
because he was also, perversely, dealing in live Grevy's
zebra. These he caught strictly on demand, as he was
always proud to claim that he never speculated on the
capture of wild animals but caught each one to a specific
order from a far-off zoological collection in Europe,
America or even Asia.
For it was in 1967 that the same Don Hunt who set out to
single-handedly 'save' the Grevy's zebra from extinction in
Kenya, also set up a company called the 'International
Animal Exchange' – henceforth known as IAE – trading
out of Ferndale, Michigan, USA, but with an office in
Nanyuki, Kenya, right next door to his game ranch at
Mount Kenya. By 1970, Don Hunt's IAE had become the
biggest commercial wild animal dealer in the world,
cornering a massive 75% of all the wild-caught animal

trade worldwide, and supplying zoos, safari parks, game parks and other zoological institutions right across the globe, netting a staggering $36 million in today's money, in that year alone.

In the dirty and murky world of animal dealers and traders, the International Animal Exchange was popularly known as 'Ferndale', so it is interesting to note that in the 'International Stud Book for Grevy's Zebra' - henceforth known as the ISB - that in the same years; 1964 and 1977, that Don Hunt was given permits to capture Grevy's zebra by the Kenyan Wildlife Service, to 'save' them from extinction by moving them to 'safer' areas; suddenly and hey presto 'Ferndale'; appears in the studbook as a major supplier of Grevy's zebra to zoological institutions worldwide.

In Don Hunt's statement made to the press in 1977 - that although the Kenya Wildlife Service had offered him the opportunity to capture and to privately sell to zoological collections the equivalent number of animals as the number that he was moving for their own 'safety', he remained adamant that these animals would not be, and were never, Grevy's zebra.

However, that is a little white lie from Don Hunt because he took a break from catching rhinos in Maralal in that year and told the vet, Jerry Haigh, that he had to catch "a few Grevy's to fulfil an order he had on his books from a zoo in Europe", which he promptly did. In fact he had a similar arrangement with the Kenya Wildlife Service that for every rhino he translocated within Kenya to 'save it from poaching' he was allowed to capture and export another rhino to the USA or Europe.

The net result of which, was the tragic death of every rhino he translocated to Meru to 'save' them from poachers. This still though, begs the question: 'So where did Don Hunt find the minimum of 52 Grevy's zebra that he exported out of Kenya between 1967 and 1976 under his trading name of 'Ferndale'?' Perhaps, one is tempted to suggest, from the 'Nairobi Orphanage' that he and his wife Iris established at their game ranch by Mount Kenya, to house young wild animals rescued "from the brink of death"?

Well, certainly eight more Grevy's zebra exported from Kenya in 1962 and 1966 - four of them to San Antonio Zoo - carry their abbreviated origins in the ISB as 'Nair Orph', referring to the animal orphanage established by the Hunts at their game ranch. They appear to have been aided and abetted by their good friends and fellow animal dealers John Seago and Tony Parkinson, who were also based in Kenya at the time. Additionally, three more Grevy's zebra were exported from the Hunt's quarantine station in Mombasa in those years but in the ISB their source is listed as 'Seago'. Perhaps demonstrating that these dealers were intimately connected in this trade and were possibly and very cleverly using each other to overcome quota or other restrictions imposed by the Kenyan government on the capture or export of Grevy's zebra at that time?

Of course, the facts and figures given above – quoted from the ISB for Grevy's zebra – may only represent the tip of a much bigger iceberg floating beneath the surface that we know nothing about, as the origins of many of the Grevy's at that time are listed as 'unknown' or their fates have been euphemistically termed by the compilers of the ISB as 'lost-to-follow-up'.

This means that the origins or the destinations of the animals remain unreported and their subsequent deaths are unrecorded, but they probably ended their days at either a circus - the name 'Chilworth' in the ISB being a surrogate address for the Chipperfield circus organisation - or perhaps even more sinisterly, at what are called 'canned' game ranches in the USA or elsewhere.

Don Hunt has a lot to answer for concerning the sudden demise of the Grevy's zebra in East Africa at that time, especially because of the four 'safari' style parks he developed in America, where many wild-caught East African ungulates and other animals became 'lost-to-follow-up' in his elaborate paper trail of deception. Not the least of which, were large groups of rhinos that just simply disappeared from history in his 'Lion Country Safari Park' which was still in use as a 'holding facility' for his massive wild animal shipments as late as 1995. That is some very dirty history indeed, of the destruction of East African wildlife, while he was supposedly championing their cause as a 'conservationist'.

Selling wild caught Grevy's zebra foals from his 'orphanage' at Mount Kenya, was already a blatant scam, as he had probably orphaned the foals himself anyway, in his desire to profit from the capture of the last members of this rapidly disappearing species.

It is a matter of public record that this is exactly what Don Hunt did with both rhinos and elephants, using a 'friendly' police helicopter and pilot to split up mothers and calves by harassing them from the air, then quickly grabbing the youngsters from a truck while the helicopter kept the confused mother away. So one could assume that he used a similar technique to grab Grevy's zebra foals, that he then kept at the "Nairobi Orphanage".

Cosy press photos of the time show both Don Hunt and his wife Iris, lovingly nurturing baby elephants, rhinos, zebras and a wide variety of other African mammals, with bottles of milk and the like, but the truth of the matter was that this so-called 'orphanage' was actually the central hub of a massive trade in not only the local wildlife, but also a vast number of exotic animals that were imported into Kenya by the Hunts. For instance, the very rare lemurs from Madagascar that they kept there in quarantine before selling them on to zoos and collectors in the USA and elsewhere.

Any remaining doubts about Don Hunt's true purpose in dabbling in 'wildlife conservation' can be comfortably laid to rest when we examine the testimony of the vet. Jerry Haigh, who was asked by Don Hunt to spend "a few weeks" - that would have actually been eight weeks as dictated by USA quarantine laws - down at the Mombasa quarantine station, to carry out the mandatory health checks that were needed for the import certificates into the USA for the sixty African ungulates that Don Hunt had captured, to order, for zoological collections there. What the vet found waiting for him at the Mombasa quarantine station was truly astonishing back then in 1970, for he was looking at a group of sixty extremely endangered African ungulates, worth well in excess of a million US dollars at that time – which today would represent five million US dollars.

Amongst these animals were seven of the very rare, almost mythical bongo antelope, highly prized by zoos all over the world, which Don Hunt personally told Jerry Haigh he had already sold to American zoos at a cool $100,000 each! It was common knowledge in the zoo world at that time, that the going rate for either a Eastern Mountain bongo, or the equally rare Okapi, was $100,000. So in bongo antelope alone, the shipment represented $700,000 to Don Hunt and his partners Seago and Parkinson. Then there were the diminutive, very shy and almost unknown Duiker forest antelope which Don Hunt had somehow transported down from the Ivory Coast of West Africa; these being Zebra-Duiker and the Yellow-Backed Duiker.

The real showpiece of this unique collection of West African ungulates, held in a dark, dingy and dismal East African quarantine station, was an almost unknown Jentink's Duiker, classified at that particular time by the IUCN as the rarest antelope in the entire world.

A closer look at Don Hunt's exotic shipment of extremely rare African ungulates to America in 1970, reveals some very remarkable details indeed and some extraordinary connections, as this shipment of bongo and other antelope was actually orchestrated by Hunt's fellow dealers, John Seago and his business partner Tony Parkinson. These men were operating in the Kenyan highlands with not only the full sanction and approval of the Smithsonian Institute of the USA but were also being funded by the much vaunted and highly respected National Geographic Society of America, who were providing the US dollars to fund this parlous, and incredibly dubious venture. This was inspired by the desire of the Director of the National Zoo in Washington to have a few bongos to show to his rapidly diminishing audience of zoo visitors, after the appalling death of an infant girl mauled by a lion. Step forward Theodore H. Reed, who convinced the National Geographic Society that John Seago - of all people – would:

"undertake an intensive survey of bongos in the wild while he captured them, and that the captive breeding programme at the Washington Zoo would save the bongo from the brink of extinction".

That was the 'official' version presented by Reed and Seago to the National Geographic Society to convince them to fund the tragic events that were about to unfold, but in private correspondence between Reed and Seago at that time – still held in the Smithsonian Institute archives – we quickly see what was actually going on: John Seago warned Reed that not all the bongos would ultimately survive this ordeal - and for once Seago had right on his side. Reed replied to Seago that all this nonsense about 'captive breeding' was just 'glop' to get the money out of the National Geographic Society, and that all he wanted was a bongo in the National Zoo at Washington to counter the bad publicity that the death of the young child had caused him.

What followed the arrival of four bongos in Washington was almost predictable; the breeding male bongo, Thugi, was killed a year later by a rhino, who 'broke' though a gate; the first bongo calf to be born died from a 'dietary deficiency' - which means it was probably a preventable death - and one of the two females, L'Ehania, was unable to carry her calves to full term.

This was a wayward and unprincipled experiment that probably cost the National Geographic Society and Smithsonian Institute a cool million US dollars; but also very likely delivered a final and fatal blow to the wild bongo population, from which it never recovered. Both Seago and Reed were very careful never to mention any details about bongos that might have died during the capture operation, the subsequent transfer to base camp, the transition to a captive diet, or the transfers to Nairobi and then to Mombasa Quarantine Station for a further sixty days. We know from the evidence of vet. Jerry Haigh that at least one of the mature bongos almost died from fluid on the lungs in quarantine in Mombasa - and the long and often deadly sea voyage to the USA to be followed by another 30 days quarantine at the Clifton facility in New York, would have taken a further toll. Seago admitted in an interview to the East African Wildlife Society in 1971, that they had needed to make urgent modifications to their methods of trapping bongos in the Kenyan highlands because of their inadequate facilities, which had resulted in the "loss" of an unknown number of animals.

This "loss" is confirmed by another animal trapper, Alan Root, who was successfully catching bongo in the same areas of the Aberdare National Park at that time, when he talks of the 'total loss' of every single bongo that other trappers caught, because of their reckless use of nylon snares, pit traps, lassos and even chemical tranquilisers while the animals were held at bay by packs of dogs, compounded by their hasty attempts to get the captured animals down out of the mountains as quickly as they could and into quarantine, to appease their American financiers. Seago's statement to the East African Wildlife Society strongly mirrors Alan Root's statement concerning Seago's success rate, when he says that "every bongo had died and the operations halted".

This also usefully confirms the failure of an initial attempt in 1968, as permits were issued by the Department of Wildlife but never fulfilled.

However, the vet, Jerry Haigh, was employed by Don Hunt in Mombasa to take the mandatory two blood samples, separated by a 30-day period, required by the USA authorities, from seven bongos. The problem being, of course, that only four bongos eventually arrived alive after their protracted journey to the Washington National Zoo. So what happened to the other three?

We know from an exchange of private correspondence between Seago and Reed as early as 1958, that the two of them were producing fraudulent orders, supposedly from 'respectable' zoos, so that additional animals could be trapped under licence and then sold on the private market to dealers and ranchers in the USA. Thus enabling William Holden to supply ranches in Texas with bongos that appeared to have paperwork approved by one of these 'respectable' zoos.

Seago and Reed's efforts to have the first bongos in the US were actually thwarted by the intrepid Alan Root who pipped them to the post by sending a pair of wild-caught bongo to Milwaukee Zoo in 1969! However, the fact that a number of trappers were operating in the Aberdares at exactly the same time, decimating the precarious wild population, and exporting the animals to the USA, causes some confusion as to the identities and origins of individual bongos. So Reed got his four bongos, Milwaukee got their two, while for now the remaining three are 'lost to follow up'.

'Captive breeding' at its absolute apex, and a debacle by all accounts when one considers that the rare bongos were captured and imported at the behest of the director of the National Zoo of Washington, Theodore H. Reed, using funds supplied by the National Geographic Society! This was a publicity stunt to lessen the impact that had been generated by the public mauling and death of a child by a lion in his zoo, which showed that the safety procedures at the zoo were inadequate. Then this same zoo director, shortly afterwards, sacrificed Don Hunt's $100,000 male bongo in another incident, when the male rhino in the next stall broke down a door and killed him! The irony of this ill-matched encounter between the bongo and powerful rhino, was that John Seago had supplied both killer and victim. One is tempted to suggest that this zoo director should have been removed from his governmental position of authority for gross negligence and charged with manslaughter for the death of the child, which occurred on his watch.

However, to compound his incompetence, Theodore H. Reed went ahead with Seago, Parkinson and Hunt's reckless and ruthless plan to intermarry two quite distinct sub-species of bongo - regardless of the dramatic influence this might have on all captive bred bongos of the future - by placing the female Western Lowland bongo from West Africa, which they called L'Ehania, as a potential mating partner for the male Eastern Mountain bongo, named Thugi.

This, of course, would have resulted in hybrids of two quite distinct sub-species which would never have met in the wild, having been separated by the vast continent of Africa for aeons.

Eastern Mountain bongo are a relic population which became isolated in the Kenyan highlands in an interglacial epoch and have become adapted to life in rare pockets two to three thousand meters above sea-level, unlike the Western Lowland bongos that thrive in far less elevated forests.

Despite the very best efforts of Theodore H. Reed of the National Zoo of Washington, the National Geographic Society, and the Smithsonian Institute to produce such an awkward zoological hybrid, they were eventually thwarted by the rhino that killed Thugi and the refusal of L'Ehania to actually give birth to any of Thugi's offspring.

Theodore H. Reed was unrepentant about his efforts to obtain wild caught bongos for the Washington National Zoo, in partnership with the likes of animal trappers such as Seago, Parkinson and Hunt, as is obvious from this 1975 'gloss' that he painted on top of his 1969 'glop' in a report to the National Geographic Society on his 'Grant number 697':

"Thus the National Geographic Society project to capture the bongos in their natural environment, along with their subsequent breeding history and the survival of their offspring at the National Zoological Park, has been gratifyingly successful."

That is the pure 'glop' of 'captive breeding' as advocated by the likes of John Knowles and Theodore H. Reed who just wanted the kudos of exotic, vanishingly rare animals to polish the image of their zoos. If the entire enterprise had been as successful as he claimed to his financiers, the National Geographic Society, then why did Reed and his Washington National Zoo need to buy three more wild bongo from the wildlife film maker, Alan Root, a couple of years later, as attested to by Root in his 1973 wildlife documentary called 'Box me a Bongo'?

As we have already seen, some discrepancies still exist. Seago suggests that he caught four bongos in Kenya on behalf of the National Zoo of Washington. However, in the private correspondence between the two men, held in the Smithsonian Institute, Seago only ever mentions two wild caught "Kenyan" bongos, raising the suspicion, of course, that at least one of these four so-called 'Eastern Mountain bongos' was in fact a Western Lowland bongo from the Ivory Coast.

Even this does not tally with the seven bongos that the vet, Jerry Haigh, found in residence at the Mombasa Quarantine Station when he went to examine them and take blood samples in 1970.

This discrepancy might well also be accounted for by the mysterious airlift, operated by the triad of Seago-Parkinson-Hunt, when they chartered an aircraft on the 24 August 1969 to fly a large number of wild caught forest antelope from the Ivory Coast to Nairobi, with an extraordinary diversion to Zurich in the opposite direction, where perhaps some, including specimens of the Western Lowland bongo, may have been unloaded, destined for European or even American zoos? It seems that this mysterious flight from the Ivory Coast was where Hunt's Gentink's Duiker - the rarest antelope in the world at that time - and the other Duikers originated, as the vet. Jerry Haigh, was specifically told by the quarantine supervisor, Haji Issak, that the Duikers had come down from the Ivory Coast.

What is also disturbing though, is that it appears to be common knowledge throughout the American zoo world, that in the late '60s and early '70s, 36 bongo (some sources indicate a number as high as 60, and others the staggering figure of 140 animals) were shipped from Kenya to the USA by both Don Hunt and William Holden - Hollywood film star and Hunt's business partner. Holden is mentioned casually as their main supplier of bongo by one of the largest 'canned' game ranches in the USA. These animals were destined for various American zoos, but there appears to be no official documentation whatsoever for these 36 (or 60 or even 140) bongos. The only easily accessible records appear to indicate a single shipment, in 1970, of four bongos from Kenya to the National Zoo of Washington. The four bongo for the National Zoo of Washington were:

'Kigai'; a three-quarters grown male, aged between 16 and 18 months, who was said to have been captured in the Aberdares, East Africa, on May 20 1969 and was later treated by the vet, Jerry Haigh, at the Mombasa Quarantine Station.   Kept at the Hunt's 'orphanage', he became sickly in July of 1969 and was later treated by Jerry Haigh, who avowed that all the bongos were in fact, of West African origin.

'Thugi'; a large adult male, who was said to have been captured in the Aberdares, East Africa, on October 7 1969. He arrived at the 'orphanage' in late November 1969, along with the female 'Kanitia'.

'Kanitia'; a young female of approximately 18 to 24 months, said to have been taken in the Aberdares, East Africa, on 22 September 1969.

'L'Ehania'; a very young female of 3 months when captured in the Ivory Coast, a Western Lowland bongo who was flown to the 'orphanage' on 24 August 1969, when 8 months old.

All four bongo were held at the Hunt's "Nairobi Orphanage" for approximately one year, before being transferred to the MQS in June 1970.

They were subsequently shipped out to the USA in August 1970, eventually arriving at the National Zoo of Washington on October 26,1970.

However, despite this detailed information about these four animals, in the ISB for Eastern Mountain bongo it is possible to find 53 animals in zoos that were very likely trapped in the wild between 1970 and 1975. All of the American zoos currently holding bongos claim proudly that all of their circa. 500 bongos are descended from this original import of wild-caught bongos trapped by Hunt, Holden, Seago and Parkinson - and then later by Alan Root - in the Aberdare forest of Mount Kenya, East Africa.

If all of the American herd are, in fact, descended from

those original shipments, as we know that at least one original animal, L'Ehania, was a Western Lowland Bongo from the Ivory Coast, why is she and every other bongo in the American herd included in the International Studbook for Eastern Mountain Bongo?

That one little Western Lowland bongo called L'Ehania is probably the biggest elephant in the narrow room of the zoological world of captive breeding and conservation.

The capture and export of these wild bongos to the USA and elsewhere, by these 'Western' animal dealers and trappers between 1968 and 1973, was actually the direct cause of uncomfortable questions being posed to the Kenyan Minister of Tourism and Wildlife by a native representative, Mr Muthania, of the Kenyan National Assembly, on the 15 July 1970, who was highly concerned at what he saw as the reckless exploitation of these rare and endangered animals by foreign interests.

These concerns were rejected by the Minister, Mr Shako, who reassured the member of the house that although rare, the bongo population of Kenya was actually not endangered, and his department only issued capture permits to licensed animal dealers after careful consideration by the 'Capture Committee' established for that very purpose. The Minister also stated that out of 15 capture licences issued by his Ministry between January 1969 and June 1970, only 12 bongos had actually been captured and that the Kenyan bongo population was "viable enough" to supply such a demand from zoological collections in the USA and elsewhere.

However the good Minister was not taking into account the number of shooting licences issued in the preceding years to big game hunters – which, according to Michael Prettejohn, was estimated to be circa 45 per year. However, an American trophy hunter, Martin Anderson, speaking of his own experiences hunting bongo in the Aberdares with Michael Prettejohn, says that in the '50s and '60s, there were, on average, 200 non-resident full licences to kill bongo issued every year and approximately 500 resident licences, giving a disturbing total of some 700 shooting licences issued by the Kenyan Wildlife Service to kill bongos purely for trophies. Although many of these licences may not have been fulfilled, it does illustrate the alarmingly casual attitude of the Kenyan authorities - this applies to pre- and post-colonial administration - towards this   rare and elusive animal, considered to be critically endangered from at least 1906, when the original remit was set for the foundation of the Kenyan Wildlife Service. These facts nullify the common perception that native 'poachers' were responsible for the decline of bongos, when in fact the local tribes actually revered the bongo and protected them. Similarly, the popularly held opinion that the 1962 Rinderpest epidemic had catastrophically reduced the population of Aberdare bongos, is totally unfounded, as although Mount Kenya's bongos were severely affected, the isolated Aberdare bongos were left completely untouched by the epidemic.

What is surprising, in this very early parliamentary confrontation between native Kenyan's and the Western trappers and dealers operating in Kenya during 1970, is the identity of the trapper who had been the cause of this debate, after he captured four wild bongo - with the required permits - and immediately air freighted them out of Kenya to Germany and the USA.

For this was none other than the later world-class wildlife documentary film-maker Alan Root, whose history reveals him to be, not only the designer of the first successful bongo trap that John Seago quickly embraced after his earlier failures to 'bring 'em back alive' but also the very first private individual in the world to hand-rear a wild caught bongo.

She was only a week old when she came into his hands in May of 1958 and he successfully kept her in captivity - in his bedroom in Kenya, of all places - until she was a year old. 'Karen', as she was called, and Alan Root, were not only flown first class to America, but he was also paid a very handsome sum of dollars for 'Karen', by the Cleveland Zoo, in order for them to be able to proudly claim, in July of 1959, to be the only zoo in the world to have an Eastern Mountain bongo.

The valid documentation of these disparate events would prove to be a most revealing exercise that one feels the current studbook keeper of the ISB for Eastern Mountain bongos should pursue relentlessly to establish the origins and legitimacy of these bongos supplied to the zoos of America by Hunt, Holden, Seago, Parkinson and Alan Root, in the '60s and '70s.

There is ample evidence around now, showing that John Seago was operating at that time in Uganda as well as Kenya, catching rare ungulates for the zoo market. The importance of this is, that very recently, in 2018, a remote wildlife monitoring camera located in the Semuliki National Park - which straddles the border between Uganda and the Democratic Republic of Congo - captured the image of a Western Lowland bongo in a country, Uganda, where it was thought never to have occurred. So perhaps John Seago and Don Hunt knew better than the Ugandan wildlife authorities about the wildlife they had there in colonial times? If that is the case, it may mean that it is entirely possible that Hunt and Co. could have caught Western Lowland bongo in Uganda in those early years, and called them Eastern Mountain bongo, because these professional animal trappers would have been acutely aware at that time, that bongo had been sighted in the Mount Elgon National Park. This National Park straddles the borders of Kenya and Uganda, making it the ideal geographical partner to have formed a 'bridge' linking the two sub-species of bongo to the corresponding Semuliki National Park on the borders of the Democratic Republic of Congo and Uganda.

All of this wildlife trafficking is really not in the remit of someone, like Don Hunt, who had set himself up as a champion and protector of the wild animals that he took under his personal control in his animal 'orphanage' at Mount Kenya Game Ranch, both of which are still operational today under the new name of 'Mount Kenya Wildlife Conservancy'. They still use Hunt's original logo for the organisation, a pair of mounted trophy bongo heads; which just about sums up Don Hunt's reckless and greedy dealings with Kenyan wildlife for almost four decades. Don Hunt in particular, seemed to have been driven by pure greed and financial avarice, with a total disregard for the wildlife of East Africa which he claimed to be 'protecting' from poachers, when he was, in fact, the biggest poacher of them all. This is confirmed by the fact that he also shipped out large numbers of primates and other monkeys to Europe and America for 'pharmaceutical' research. Just in 1978 alone, Don Hunt's IAE shipped 248 baboons out of Kenya to the USA for such research.
Hardly the actions of a man committed to the preservation of the wildlife of East Africa.
It is a useful exercise to compare what Don Hunt privately boasted to the vet, Jerry Haigh, in 1969, about his

commercial interests in the rare bongo antelope that he had at his quarantine station in Mombasa; that "they had been sold by 'us' to American zoos for $100,000 each" and then compare that with his press 'glop' to a reporter from the Voice of America, 35 years later when he claimed that he was entirely responsible for saving the bongo from the "brink of extinction":

"You could see the bongo were going to be overwhelmed by this human population explosion," he said. "So we got together with the Kenyan government and made a deal with them that we would purchase 20 bongos from them and we would send them off to the States so that there would be a gene pool there."

There was no 'deal' with the Kenyan government, who had had actually revoked Don Hunt's MKGR animal dealer licences, and had refused to issue new permits because of grave concerns about the activities of his International Animal Exchange enterprise.

Of course, Don Hunt also avoids mentioning that his partners in this bongo 'get rich quick' scheme, Seago and Parkinson, who were still licensed even though Don Hunt was not, only paid the Kenyan government a pathetic total of $1,280 for 20 bongo export permits but then made a whopping 2 million US dollars upon the sale of the animals to American zoos. That is how Don Hunt and the Kenyan government "got together" to make a "deal".

"Despicable!" would be a mild comment, given that it is now common knowledge that many of the bongo that Hunt, Seago and Parkinson trapped in the mountainous Aberdare National Park, died before they could get them down the slopes. It is difficult to obtain exact figures, as these animal trappers are very reluctant to admit to, or record, the attrition rates that accompanied their reckless methods; but the Kenyan Minister for Wildlife in the trapping season of 1969/1970 - reported to the House of Representatives that a total of 15 licences had been issued for the trapping of bongo, and that 12 of these licenses had been fulfilled. Given that we only have records of six bongos being successfully captured in the Aberdares in that period, four of them by Alan Root, and two by Seago and Parkinson, it might be possible to speculate that the other six bongo died in the capture process.

Alan Root appears to confirm this when he is highly critical of the primitive capture methods employed by the other trappers operating in the Aberdares at the same time as he was. The only other trappers there were Seago, Parkinson and Hunt.

The highly respected bongo specialist, Michael Prettejohn, in his own account of those days in Kenya, 'Endless Horizons', mentions the role of one of his own trackers, Peter Mwangi, who worked with Hunt and Seago, trapping bongos on behalf of zoos in Europe and America in the Abedares, in the late 1960s to early 1970s.

Prettejohn confirms that a total of 50 animals were captured and subsequently exported to those zoos; but importantly, he also states that "only 50% of the bongo captured in this operation survived", meaning that for every live bongo that Hunt and Seago captured for zoos, they left one dead bongo behind them.

Taking that figure of 100 animals, either exported or left dead in the forest by Hunt and Seago, adding the 36 bongo that Alan Root captured in the same area around the same time, one is then able to see what a dramatic and fatal impact this would have had on the remaining, highly fragile population of around 370 Aberdare wild bongo.

Stripped in one year of more than a quarter of their number to supply the greedy and insatiable desire of the zoos of the world for even more wild bongo. That is shameful!

Alan Root doesn't give a lot away in his own memoires concerning his capture of bongo in the Aberdares but his long-suffering wife, Joan, was more forthcoming in her own correspondence. She detailed that together, they captured a total of 30 bongo, which they then kept at their dedicated quarantine facility at Lake Naivasha, where 6 calves were subsequently born, bringing the total of exported bongo to 36. Joan Root mentions that the mother of the first calf born there, was captured in early May of 1969 along with 3 others.

That this trapping of bongo in the Aberdares had been a long-term project is shown by a cable that the Roots received from Milwaukee Zoo in September of 1969, confirming the arrival of 2 bongos at the Clifton facility in New Jersey, where they spent a month, before being moved on to Milwaukee Zoo. In addition, it seems likely that the bongo calf born at the National Zoo of Washington in April of 1974 was the result of breeding between 2 of the Root's bongos, as it was called 'Naivasha' after the Root's holding facility by that lake in Kenya.

It is worth comparing what Alan Root said in 2009 of his bongo trapping exploits in the Aberdares, to the earlier comments made by Don Hunt in 2004 about his own dealings with this rare antelope, as both men appeared to be attempting to justify the unjustifiable, many years after their somewhat mercenary campaigns to exploit the few remaining bongo left in the Aberdares in the late 60's:

"By sending bongos to zoos around the world, they would establish a breeding pool of bongos in zoos, so the wild population would never again be jeopardised. Thus the species would be both recognised and preserved."

Now that is 'glop', because Alan Root - just like Don Hunt - admits that the sale of the bongos that he captured for those zoological collections, made him an enormous amount of money, which he then used to buy helicopters, light planes, many vehicles and properties all over the world, as well as financing the famous wildlife documentaries that he made for the BBC and others. He was only paid £2,000 sterling by the BBC for each film he made – a year's work – but the going rate was up to $100,000 for every one of the 36 bongos he sold to zoos, making him some 3.6 million US dollars for a year's work. So the noble and altruistic motives that both men attribute to their capture of the few remaining bongos left in the Aberdares in 1969, can perhaps be dismissed in favour of the vast fortunes they both made from exploiting those rare animals for commercial gain.

Even if their altruistic motives were genuine, history has shown those motives to be seriously misguided and inherently false. A recent DNA analysis of the remaining scant population of wild bongo in the Aberdares indicates a genetic diversity of up to 95% greater today than the captive zoo population that Hunt, Seago, Parkinson and Root established way back in 1969. This is a clear demonstration of the failure of 'captive breeding' as a tool of conservation in the real world, whereas it seems to work wonders in the world of zoological 'glop'. A failure, simply because that 'captive breeding programme' has resulted in the deadly genetic 'bottleneck' of extinction, guaranteed by the fractured and fragmented nature of modern zoo husbandry.

The fact of the matter is, that we will probably never know how many bongos ended up in the illicit possession of the Hunt's at their 'orphanage' at the MKGR. Illicit because it was in that year that Don Hunt was forced to relinquish his IAE animal dealer permit, and his subsequent application for a new animal dealer permit in the name of the MKGR was rejected by the 'Capture Committee' of the Kenyan Wildlife Service. Thereby, any animals he trapped in those years – and this includes the bongos and Grevy's zebra - were trapped without authorization from the KWS and would have been in his possession illegitimately. They would have been, quite simply, 'poached' and Don Hunt was the greatest poacher of them all.

This is dramatically illustrated in official Kenyan government documents that still exist, thanks to the ruthless determination of probably one of the greatest unsung heroes of that colonial age in East Africa, Ian Parker. He was a former game warden, whose relentless efforts to right the wrongs that the likes of Don Hunt and other Western ranchers had visited upon the fragile eco-system and its endangered wildlife, are perhaps the only positive element to have survived the catastrophic impact of the colonial government in East Africa.

A document called 'The Affair of the Grevy's Zebra', prepared by the Kenyan Wildlife Service in the '60s and '70s, conclusively shows Don Hunt and his fellow animal trappers, like Seago and Parkinson, in their true colours; operating in a shadowy underworld of bribery and corruption with strong links to the trade in endangered animals, and perhaps even to the illegal trade in ivory and rhino horns, with gangs of 'game wardens' slaughtering the very animals that they were employed to protect; the elephants and rhinos.

This was all under the protective umbrella of the Kenyan Wildlife Service through the influence of a corrupt employee, J.M. Kariuki, the assistant minister of Tourism and Wildlife, with whom Don Hunt had a 'special' relationship which allowed him to do just about anything he liked.

Just one of Parker's many preserved documents shows the astonishing level of Don Hunt's declared trading as the MKGR, in the wildlife of Kenya. However, this is only his official declaration, which does not take into account all of the animals he was able to capture and export without declaring them to the KWS. In 1978 alone, Hunt's MKGR capture and export declaration featured:

"60 gerenuk; 9 duiker; 70 dik-dik; 47 kudu; 53 topi; 30 hartebeeste; 61 Grevy's zebra; 30 bongo; 64 giraffe; 20 rhino and 48 elephants".

So in all, Don Hunt, as the IAE, shipped out a recorded 1,043 wild animals in 1978, including those 492 ungulates, fulfilling orders from greedy and insatiable zoos, claiming to Kenyan government officials that he had only made a mere £350,000 sterling on the sale of all these wild caught animals to zoos in the USA and elsewhere. Even in Parker's preserved document we can see that Don Hunt claims that the sale of a job-lot of 30 bongos had only netted him the paltry sum of £60,000, that is £2,000 per bongo. However, we have the published testimony of the vet. Jerry Haigh, having processed those very bongos through the strict quarantine requirements demanded by the USA, who emphatically reports that Don Hunt told him that he was being paid $100,000 for each bongo he delivered alive to an American zoo. That makes a cool 3 million dollars in bongo alone that year, so Don Hunt was paid somewhere between 5 and 10 million US dollars just for the ungulates, not his claimed £350,000 sterling for the whole year's animal dealing. What Western trappers like Don Hunt and John Seago declared they were doing was entirely different to what they actually did.

Again, the only reasonable explanation for Don Hunt to declare the value of the 30 bongos at £2,000 per animal, could be that they were, in fact, the much less valuable and far more numerous Western Lowland sub-species, which he had clandestinely imported from the Ivory Coast in his 'Flying Ark'.

The report on "The Affair of the Grevy's Zebra" then goes into some of the details of the scam that Don Hunt was enacting with the connivance and cooperation of some of the most senior game wardens of the Kenyan Wildlife Service and the assistant Minister of Tourism and Wildlife,

J.M. Kariuki.

Much of this information was compiled secretly by Major Rodney Elliot of the Game Department, but acting very carefully because his immediate superior, Chief Game Warden Mutinda, was not only implicated in the scam, but was also closely related, by family, to other officials of the Game Department, who were also being actively monitored along with Don Hunt and others, and were allegedly involved in the trade of not only endangered animals but also in the lucrative and illegal trade in ivory and rhino horn.

The entire scam between Don Hunt of the MKGR and J.M. Kariuki, assistant Minister of Tourism and Wildlife, was suspected when the 'Capture Committee' of the ministry became highly concerned about reports of Don Hunt and his IAE "having a reputation for very shady dealing", following several reports in the late '60s about IAE's illicit activities. Not the least of which, was Hunt's blatant animal dealing from the Nairobi 'Orphanage' and the Mount Kenya Game Ranch, which he claimed was a 'conservation' project. In late 1969, the 'Capture Committee' - official title "Advisory Committee for the Capture and Export of Wild Animals" - made it quite clear that they had finally had enough of Don Hunt and his IAE and became very uncooperative in the issuing of capture permits.

Don Hunt's answer was to notify the 'Capture Committee', in early 1970, that he had ceased trading as the IAE and that his dealer's permit - issued by the C.C. - should be cancelled in that name. He then immediately applied to the C.C. for a dealer's permit in the name of the Mount Kenya Game Ranch, fully expecting it to be granted because of his close ties to the senior officials of the Game Department.

But he was dealing with a very tough individual indeed on the C.C., Richard Leaky. Leaky absolutely refused to consider the application because of Hunt's 'shady dealings' on the black market and then went on to ask some very awkward questions about his activities as an unlicensed animal dealer, catching animals without permits issued by the 'Capture Committee'.

Among Leaky's awkward questions were:
Why was Don Hunt trapping 20 Hunter's antelope a year when he had no permit and no license?
Why was Don Hunt being issued with permits by senior members of the Game Department who had no right to issue such permits, as this was solely the remit of the 'Capture Committee'?
Why was Don Hunt not being charged the usual fee of 8,000 Kenyan shillings for legal capture permits, but instead was being charged a nominal fee of two shillings, or in some cases, no charge?
How could an individual like Don Hunt capture many groups of Grevy's zebra at that time period - separate permits were issued for 24 Grevy's; 9 Grevy's; 16 Grevy's; 30 Grevy's; 20 Grevy's; 5 Grevy's; 4 Grevy's - when firstly, he had no animal dealer's license, which was a legal requirement, and secondly, he had not been issued with the relevant permits by the 'Capture Committee'?
The answer to all of those awkward questions is that Don Hunt had the full support of three of the highest officials in the Game Department and Ministry of Tourism and Wildlife, one of these being Chief Game Warden Mutindi, who had made an unprecedented, extraordinary personal appearance before the 'Capture Committee', appealing for them to issue a full animal dealer's permit to Don Hunt and the Mount Kenya Game Ranch. An appeal they flatly refused.
At the same time, a written appeal was made to the C.C. by another senior game warden, Henry Mulandi, indicating that Don Hunt and the MKGR had the full support of the

Game Department for the issuing of such a permit. This was again refused.

It so happens that Major Rodney Elliot was, at this time, investigating both these senior officers of the Game Department, for their active roles in the widespread poaching of endangered species, by game rangers under their direct control, and also for their suspected links to the illegal ivory trade. Elliot was astonished to find in his investigations, that the senior game warden Mulandi had actually set up his own animal dealing company (shades of Don Hunt's IAE, perhaps?), dealing in rare and endangered East African wildlife, appropriately called 'Animal Farm', with a business address in Holland but a telephone number and post office box in Nairobi.

This ambition to profit from the lucrative trade of East African wildlife went right up to the top, as Don Hunt and the assistant Minister of Tourism and Wildlife, J.M. Kariuki, held hands on the development of a private ranch near Gilgil in the Rift Valley, which they jointly planned to turn into a 'game reserve'.

The assistant Minister Kariuki gleefully issued Don Hunt with illegitimate permits to catch just about anything he liked, as long as some of the animals ended up on his private game 'reserve'; and that is exactly what the two bandits did.

Don Hunt suddenly found himself in some kind of animal trapper's heaven, where he could do just what the hell he liked, when the hell he liked, and how the hell he liked; and this coincides with the exact time that all those bongo started tumbling down out of the mountains of the Aberdare National Park to land so fortuitously in his 'Nairobi Orphanage' at the MKGR.

Don Hunt's boldness and greed increased with his sudden good fortune, and instead of the historical arrangement with the Game Department; that for every animal he moved for them, he would take one animal himself for export to zoos, he suddenly increased that rate of exchange - with the aid of Mulandi and Mutindi - from 1:1 to 1:2, and a few months later to 1:3. So that for every one Grevy's zebra, or other ungulate, that he 'translocated' to the assistant Minister's private game ranch/reserve, he was taking three more animals for himself to export for profit. This obviously netted him a great deal of money.

It also earned him a written rebuke from Major Rodney Elliot, but the good Major was powerless to stop Hunt's illicit activities, as the men backing Hunt were Elliot's superior officers. But snipe he did, as in a letter of November 1969, he castigates Don Hunt for the catastrophic loss of 12 Grevy's zebra, out of a herd of 44 that he had captured and corralled so inadequately that the 12 deaths resulted from panic, shock and exhaustion. Hunt's reply was dismissive, and claimed that the loss of quarter of the herd was high, but "acceptable" in the circumstances!

Undeterred, a year later Hunt was back in the saddle, applying for permits to capture 30 more Grevy's zebra - still unlicensed - confident that he would get the permits, specifying that they were to fulfil zoo orders.

As we saw in an earlier chapter Don Hunt had struck a deal with the Game Department to translocate 140 Grevy's zebra from Isiolo to Tsavo West and Samburu, and he claimed that this was done under his usual arrangement with the KWS; that for every zebra he translocated he was permitted to capture another zebra for himself for subsequent export abroad to zoos. However, we now know from Rodney Elliot that he had subsequently upped this cosy arrangement to a 1:2 barter rate - and even at some point to a ridiculous rate of 1:3 - which would mean that his own final personal tally from this deal could have been between 280 and 420 animals.

These figures do perhaps solve a peculiar anomaly in the ISB for Grevy's zebra, where there are over 100 wild caught Grevy's recorded in the late '60s and early '70s that must have originated in Kenya but the supplier of those animals is given as 'unknown'. This can perhaps be credited to sloppy paperwork by the zoos concerned but that is relatively unimportant, as there were only three suppliers at that time in Kenya who were capable of meeting such a demand, these being Carr-Hartley, the twin team of Seago and Parkinson and, of course, Don Hunt. Given the fact that Don Hunt was the only trapper/dealer in Kenya in those years who was catching Grevy's zebra in such high numbers, it is entirely plausible that it was indeed Don Hunt who was also supplying the zoos of America and Europe with these wild caught animals of 'unknown' origin.

Owning the only quarantine station, at Mombasa, on the entire Eastern seaboard of the African continent that was approved by the American and British authorities, was obviously quite a bonus for Don Hunt.

These serendipitous circumstances could lead one to conclude that Don Hunt's trapping activities led to the sudden collapse of the Grevy's zebra population in the 1970s - from which it has never recovered - and that he may well have been responsible for the death of many thousands of zebra, in collateral damage, through his relentless and greedy pursuit of them for the zoological market.

It wasn't actually a licence to print money, but just about as close as you can get.

Another example of Hunt's reckless and ruthless exploitation of Kenya's wildlife, is graphically illustrated in extant documents of the time, which show the 'Capture Committee' seriously questioning Don Hunt's illicit annual capture of twenty of the extremely endangered Hirola or

Hunter's antelope (Beatragus hunteri). In 1978 alone he had a herd of 42 Hunter's antelope at the MKGR - which again Hunt was doing with illicitly issued permits that conveniently bypassed the 'C.C.' (minute 1938 of the 'C.C.'). Here, the 'Capture Committee' pointed out that the Hirola was considered to be the rarest antelope in the world, by both the WWF and IUCN - two international conservation organisations who had just come to an agreement with the Kenyan government to fund a nature reserve specifically to protect Hirola - and that this rare and vulnerable antelope had enjoyed the full protection of the KWS and Game Department since 1957 when all hunting and trapping (including live-trapping for zoological export) was totally banned.

Yet, here again was Don Hunt with his gang of trappers, right out in the open, flaunting the rules and regulations, and testing the law by trapping live Hirola for his so-called animal 'orphanage' right under the watchful eyes of the game wardens, who it appeared were utterly powerless to stop him. Major Rodney Elliot, a senior game warden, soon found this out when he tried to stop Hunt hunting Hunter's antelope, for the good Major Elliot was quickly transferred to the far-off coast of Kenya, which conveniently kept him quiet about Hunt and the Hunter's antelope, amongst other things.

Another clue to Don Hunt's nefarious activities in this regard, is hidden away in a collection of memoirs by former Kenyan game wardens, collated by Ian Parker and Stan Bleazard – 'An Impossible Dream' – when game warden Dave McCabe mentions a curious incident involving one of his foot-patrols; a local woman had been stopped near the 'Ukambani' border in a Land Rover, without number plates, loaded down with ivory tusks from slaughtered elephants. However she escaped arrest by producing a 'collector's permit', purportedly signed by the wife of the incumbent Kenyan president. Ian Parker commented that such "Presidential Collector's Permits" had been issued by the President's Office to ex-Mau Mau freedom fighters, to allow them to collect all the trophies they had supposedly stashed away in the many years that they were confined to the highlands of Kenya by the British Army. This was what he called "the foot in the door" for many unlicensed poachers and trappers who were awarded "Collector's permits", which neatly bypassed the efforts of the 'Capture Committee' and his own game rangers to protect the wildlife of Kenya.

We already know that Don Hunt had his foot in that door because he was acting under the direct - but illicit - authority of the Assistant Minister of Tourism and Wildlife, J.M. Kariuki, by supplying him with such animals as Hunter's antelope and Grevy's zebra for his private ranch near Gilgil. Perhaps the biggest mystery of all, is that not one of those many captured Hunter's antelope is traceable today. Their numbers are almost impossible to estimate but perhaps an estimate of 200 to 300 over the years is reasonable, as Hunt had 42 animals at the MKGR in 1978 alone and we have no record of them ever being exported for the zoo trade. Unless, of course, they were sold as a different species. If any of these extremely rare antelope ever ended up in the Texan exotic hunting ranches, or even in private zoo collections, they are being very coy about that eventuality indeed.

It might be pertinent to consider here, that the only place that one will see 'Hirola' - Hunter's antelope - today, outside of the wilds of East Africa, is in the many natural history museum dioramas all over the USA and elsewhere, where stuffed antelope are exhibited in cosy little 'family groups'. Just like the group that were shot dead for exhibition purposes by the Academy of Natural Sciences of Philadelphia in 1929. So it is entirely possible that the collection of these rare trophy animals for exhibition -

whether for live exhibition in a zoological collection, or as a dead stuffed specimen for a museum - played a large part in the eventual collapse of the already scarce wild population of Hirola. We do know that this is exactly what led to the eventual collapse of the viable wild population of giant sable antelope in Angola.

The fact is that in other trapping escapades - this time legitimate and with the approval of the 'Capture Committee', KWS and the WWF - the Hunter's antelope were trapped and relocated to areas where it was genuinely thought they might have a better chance of survival. The game wardens concerned became extremely alarmed though, by the high rates of mortality, as the antelope either died from exhaustion from the chase and capture, or shortly after in the holding pens, and even more dying on the protracted road journey to their new destination. The attrition rate was so high on such a vulnerable population of rare animals, that the game wardens sensibly halted the translocation efforts until they had perfected their capture techniques. Then they brought in Royal Navy helicopters to airlift the Hunter's antelope to their new reserve in Tsavo East.

Given this, it would appear that Don Hunt's capture attempts and subsequent husbandry of the Hunter's antelope that came under his control would have had an even higher attrition rate than that of the altruistic game wardens who had the common decency and wisdom to call a halt to their efforts when so many of the rare antelope died. However, we know now that Hunt would not have had similar morals and would have just simply ransacked the herds to get what he wanted, which was as many rare antelope rammed into his 'orphanage' as he could, in order to turn a few thousand dollars through his International Animal Exchange.

Unfortunately the plight of the Hunter's antelope has largely escaped the notice of the world of conservation - being very much a 'lost to follow up' species for them - and there is very little information on its history or status, but what is speculated is that prior to the 1970s, the population had been estimated by some sources to be as high as 10,000 to15,000 animals located in the Garissa district around the Kenyan and Somalia border-zone. That perhaps over-inflated population estimate doesn't really hold up to the eye-witness accounts of the game wardens of the time: Dave McCabe, who translocated some of the Hunter's antelope to Tsavo East in the early 1960s, described them as:

"Having a **limited** distribution in the Garissa district North of the Tana river close to the Kenyan-Somalia border."

Even as early as 1901 the Hunter's antelope appeared to be something of a rarity, with numbers that may never have equalled the population of 15,000 animals mentioned by many sources, and is today the rarest antelope in the world. The very man who first mooted the idea of a Kenyan Game Department, A. Blayney-Percival, in a 1901 letter to the Deputy Commissioner of Kenya, commented in his report on the Hunter's antelope, that it was:

"A very **local** animal found only in one **small** district on the Tana river."

Neither of the comments by these two experienced game wardens seems to support the idea of a large population of Hirola, in such a narrowly restricted range, at any time prior to the sudden drop of numbers between the '70s and '80s, when various sources estimate that there was a catastrophic 90% decline in the population. This was due mainly, it is thought, to the almost complete extirpation of elephants within that area, leading to the inevitable decrease of suitable grazing for the antelope. Consequently, bushland quickly developed without the herds of elephant that had previously managed it.

The KWS' efforts to obviate this rapid decline of the Hunter's antelope by translocation, as we have just seen, led to the deaths of many of the animals. It is important to note that game warden, Dave McCabe, remarked in his memoirs, that the main reason for the attempted relocation was the proposed damming of the Tana river which might then have flooded the Hirola's habitat. However, even when more 'user friendly' techniques were employed, the subsequent translocation attempts fizzled out, with a total of only 30 Hunter's antelope, out of a claimed several thousand animals, moved into Tsavo East, subsequent fate largely unknown. This does beg the question; if the population of Hunter's antelope was really in the thousands in the 1960s and they were threatened in their entirety as a species by the construction of a dam on the Tana river – why were only 30 of the animals successfully translocated by McCabe and his team in 1963, leaving perhaps over 5,000 Hunter's antelope to survive the expected flooding? That doesn't seem to make any sense whatsoever, especially as the river was never flooded!

In 1995, a further 76 Hirola were translocated from the same area to Tsavo East and then another 29 joined them in 1996. However, a survey in 2000, revealed a total of only 77 animals. Eleven years later, another survey revealed that the population in Tsavo East had dropped to 76 animals. However, taking into account the extremely fragile status of the remaining population of Hunter's antelope, when Don Hunt was taking out twenty animals a year in the 1970s - and perhaps even into the '80s and '90s - it may well be that he has a lot to answer for in regard to their extreme rarity, as their wild   population today stands at around 500 individuals. Yet again, another one of Don

Hunt's relentless 'lost to follow up' extinction campaigns against East African wildlife.

Fortunately, more recently, local native communities have gathered together to create a protected reserve for the remaining fragile population of Hirola. Working together with the independent conservation organisation, Terra Nuova, a predator-proof sanctuary of 23 square kilometres has been provided for 48 of this extraordinarily rare antelope, which today are breeding well in their reserve. This is a refreshing illustration of how the native communities have stepped up to save their endemic wildlife, which the exploitative Western trappers have helped to cripple by reducing the already struggling wild population to critically low levels under the pretext of "saving them from the brink of extinction".

Even today, the ruthless and careless actions of Don Hunt, John Seago and Tony Parkinson, and the similarly ruthless and careless zoo directors like Theodore H. Reed and John Knowles who funded and sponsored these trappers, are still having massive repercussions on the entirely fragile population of the few remaining Eastern Mountain bongo and Grevy's zebra in Kenya. As we have just seen, Don Hunt's former empire, the 'Mount Kenya Game Ranch', where over the years he made millions of dollars in the trade of live East African mammals through his International Animal Exchange, is today the much revamped and supposedly 'respectable' "Mount Kenya Wildlife Conservancy".

Back in 2004, this MKWC attempted to 'reintroduce' a group of ten captive-bred bongos into the highlands of Kenya, but they were stopped at the last minute by the Kenyan Wildlife Service, who had been warned by some independent scientists and researchers that these captive-bred animals might well have a totally negative genetic impact on the very scarce remaining wild population of Eastern Mountain bongos. One possible reason for the concern of the Kenyan Wildlife Service, could well be that there exists a very real danger that the captive bred bongos, which are descended from the wild specimens caught by Hunt, Seago and Parkinson, were genetically tainted by the reckless substitution of Western Lowland for the much rarer and far more lucrative Eastern Mountain bongos at the Mount Kenya Game Ranch.

It is a matter of public record that Don Hunt was holding 36 'bongo' in a compound behind the animal 'orphanage' in the years between 1977 and 1979. At the time, Hunt was proud to boast in a press interview, that he had been organising and financing expeditions to catch rare and endangered wildlife all over the vast continent of Africa for many years, and that a special commercial transport aircraft he called the 'Flying Ark' had been constantly employed to ferry live-trapped West African animals from Liberia, the Ivory Coast and Nigeria to his East African IAE base at the Mount Kenya Game Ranch. This indicates strongly that many of the bongos kept at the pens in the 'Nairobi Orphanage' at MKGR, could well have been Western Lowland bongos flown in on his 'Flying Ark'.

Given the scarcity of the Eastern Mountain bongo in the late '60s, and the almost overwhelming difficulties that Seago and Parkinson experienced attempting to trap them for Don Hunt and the American zoos, one can easily imagine the ever astute and totally commercial animal dealers going instead for the easier option of the far more common Western Lowland bongos and then merely swapping their name tags, in quarantine, for the vastly rarer Eastern Mountain bongos. Just the sort of 'hey presto' that this trio of trappers were absolute experts at.

If this is the case, it is no wonder that the Kenyan Wildlife Service acted quickly to prevent the MKWC from releasing their captive bred stock of bongos into the 'wild'. However, it must be said that the Kenyan Wildlife Service also had serious concerns about the lack of genetic material provided by the MKWC to be evaluated, and their very real fears that the captive bred American animals might well either infect wild bongos with imported diseases, or themselves be infected by the local diseases that they had never been exposed to in captivity.

A press release from the "Mount Kenya Wildlife Conservancy" shortly after this refusal by the Kenyan Wildlife Service to allow them to release their bongos commented:

"The owners of the Mount Kenya Game Ranch *(that being Don and Iris Hunt)* have saved and bred bongo antelope since 1970 entirely with private funding of its directors, until the Mount Kenya Wildlife Conservancy was formed to take over in 2004."

Two notable things about this statement, are that the first part is perhaps what we have termed 'glop'. This word was coined by zoo director Theodore H. Reed to describe his own personal dealings with bongo antelope. It is most appropriate in its application to Don Hunt, in that it is almost impossible to comment on the breeding history of the bongos kept at MKGR simply because of the failure by the Hunts to record or report events associated with their animals, specifically in regard to the bongos that they kept at the 'orphanage' over many years while they were involved in catching and dealing at their Mount Kenya

Game Ranch. Yes, existing records do appear to indicate that a few bongo (only six calves can be reliably documented in the ISB prior to 2004) might have been bred by the Hunts at the MKGR. This strikingly low number of calves is so inconsistent with other institutions' records of captive breeding Hunt-sourced wild bongo in those years - that the discrepancies inevitably point to either a serious mismanagement of the bongo herd at the MKGR, or perhaps a deliberate attempt by the Hunts to disguise the fact that they were still selling bongos well into the late 1990's to undisclosed private owners in the USA and elsewhere.

Such a scenario could explain how Dvur Kralove Zoo in the CCSR came to be the proud owners of a so-called wild caught male Eastern Mountain bongo in 2004. Despite the fact that the newly renamed Mount Kenya Wildlife Conservancy imported 18 captive-bred Eastern Mountain bongo, at great expense and fanfare, for proposed 're-introduction' into the desperately depleted and highly protected wild in that year.

In 1978 the Hunts claimed to have a bongo herd of ten animals; four males and six females, but by 2004 that herd had only increased in the intervening 26 years to a total of 18 bongo; eight males and ten females.

Meanwhile in the USA the 'officially recognised' 36 wild caught bongos that the Hunts, and others like Alan Root, had sold to zoos in the 70's had produced 400 calves by 2004.

Even more mysterious, is the claim by both the Hunts in 2004, that they had produced a total of 50 calves from their herd of ten bongo at the MKGR since 1978, but they admitted to having only 18 bongo remaining at the 'orphanage', so what happened to those 50 calves?

That is some serious 'glop'.

What we do know is that those wild-caught bongos – variously estimated as between 30, 60 and even 140 animals – that the Hunts, and others, had provided for the American and European zoo markets between 1968 and 1978, made them millions of US dollars. The influential Wall Street Journal estimated that Don Hunt's income from animal trading, in 1970 alone, was $6 million, which is the equivalent of about $36 million in current dollars.

As we have already seen, the estimated 30 bongo he had on his game ranch in that time period, at $100,000 a specimen to American zoos, would alone have given him an income of $3 million, leaving him obliged to make up any 'shortfall' with Grevy's zebra.

The fact is that those American zoos which Don Hunt had originally supplied with bongos, back in the 70's, only attempted to 'reintroduce' their captive bred stock to the Mount Kenya Game Ranch in 2004, when it became the Mount Kenya Wildlife Conservancy, albeit still owned and managed by the Hunts.

Chapter Five

Even in 2004, Don and Iris Hunt were still there at the MKWC, supervising the arrival of an airlift of captive bred American bongos which they immediately put out onto infested pasture polluted by previous livestock. This resulted in the death of four bongos within a month – three females and one male - from theileriosis, the disease caused by a tick-borne infection of Theileria. This was then later thought, by independent experts, to actually have been the similar and equally deadly tick-borne babesiosis. This disease may well have contributed to the further deaths of seven more bongo shortly after, all females. However, this information was somehow obscured by the Hunts and the MKWC at that time and still awaits final confirmation from them, with these further seven deaths being recorded as of 'unknown' causes and 'unknown' date by an investigating committee. This makes **eleven** deaths in total within a year, from a breeding stock of **eighteen** bongo imported from America.   Confusion between theileriosis and babesiosis is still relatively common even today, but both are diseases transmitted to ungulates by ticks, which, along with 'East Coast Fever', 'Tropical Theileria' and many others, are all forms of 'Piroplasmosis'. The infection in itself is mostly of minimal impact on the health of the infected ungulate, and it is usually only under overwhelming stress, of pursuit, capture and close confinement for example, that the disease develops, often resulting in the rapid death of the animal concerned. Imported, zoo-bred ungulates that have never been exposed to these 'tick-borne-infections' – henceforth known in this volume as 'TBI's' – in their artificially created environment have absolutely no immunity to the infection or the disease and are liable to succumb to the negative impact of the TBI much more readily than their wild counterparts. It must be said that the fatal impact of TBI's on zoo-bred ungulates suddenly reintroduced into a natural environment in Africa, or elsewhere, seems to have been largely ignored by the zoos and organisations concerned in these attempts, to their cost and the wasted lives of the precious, rare animals that have died as a result.

The Kenyan Wildlife Service of the time, were well used to dealing with Theileria, so it should have been easily controlled in a properly managed environment. But it wasn't, which may have contributed to the long-term illness of the few remaining bongos, resulting in the easily preventable death of most of the herd of 18 American captive bred bongo.

It is here that it is imperative to realise that the Hunts had a very long history of such disregard for the well-meant advice of the KWS and the game wardens they employed, especially when it came to the introduction of relocated wild animals into pastures previously inhabited by domestic livestock. In 1970 the indomitable Major Rodney Elliot – game warden and implacable thorn in Don Hunt's side – wrote to him warning him of the dangers of introducing wild animals, whether captive bred or wild caught, into areas previously holding domestic livestock because of the threat of infestation by ticks. This letter from Elliot to Hunt is a matter of public record, and shows conclusively that thirty-four years before the disaster of the bongo repatriation attempt in 2004, the Hunt's and their MKWC were well aware of the risks involved.

That is entirely unforgivable.

So, the imported captive-bred American bongos were almost totally wiped out - not only from a reduction in their original numbers as a viable herd but more critically, perhaps, from the severely reduced genetic potential left within the surviving animals. However, in the 1970's, their few wild Kenyan cousins held onto the last bastion of the Aberdare National Park, despite the best efforts of the zoos of the world to extirpate them by capturing more than a quarter of the remaining population of 500. Removing those animals very likely rendered the remaining population unsustainable and may well still result in their ultimate extinction.

Now that is ironic.

The awful reality of this situation was finally confirmed by Donald Bunge, the 'Wildlife and Operations Manager' of the MKWC, in a talk he gave to the 'Trackers' organisation of Kenya in August 2018 – fourteen years after the tragic event occurred - when he admitted that **all 18** of the imported captive bred American bongos had died since 2004 from 'TBI'. This admission is shocking, as although other sources acknowledge 12 deaths by 2005, as manager of the MKWC, he should know better than anyone which animals died, when and why.

But even this overdue admission was just more 'glop', as a much earlier report in 2006 by an IUCN specialist group involved in the Kenyan bongo reintroduction scheme, publicly stated that only four of the deaths of the American captive bred bongos could be attributed to 'TBI', and it appears that the remaining deaths may have been caused by poor husbandry.

Additionally, the Hunts and the MKWC had not - according to another independent report on their proposed bongo reintroduction scheme - corresponded officially with the Kenyan Wildlife Services during the years from 2002 to 2005, leaving those responsible for the conservation of the highly endangered bongo in their own country, completely in the dark about the confused intentions of the Hunts and their MKWC.

The same independent report also states that:

"There is no comprehensive plan describing the proposed reintroduction programme."

This situation could be summed up by Don Hunt's very own words in a much earlier press interview after another of his many self-created wildlife disasters:

"We really don't know what the hell we're doing!"

That particular disaster in the late '70s cost the lives of untold numbers of the magnificent Imperial zebra, the Grevy's zebra, and was probably a major factor in the sudden decline of that highly endangered species from a population in the '70s of 15,000 to 1,500 in the '80s. In that regard, it is interesting to note that the US Fish and Wildlife Service of the Department of the Interior had listed the Grevy's Zebra as a 'Threatened' species, but then in 1977 the FWS proposed to upgrade it to 'Endangered' due to data received from various sources. However, a variety of interested parties immediately produced new data suggesting that the Grevy's Zebra was in no way in danger of extinction, throughout its range. In fact, twenty-one letters were received by the FWS in regard to the change of the status of the species and eleven of them were actively against the proposal to upgrade it. Three organisations in particular wanted amendments made to the legislation so that they could utilise wild-caught Grevy's Zebras in their captive breeding programmes. Unsurprisingly, we find that the most vociferous of these was the Mount Kenya Game Park under the management of our old friend Don Hunt. This opposition was swiftly followed, in 1978, by immense pressure from the Safari Club International - very likely under the auspices of William Holden, Don Hunt's close friend and business partner in the MKGP, who claimed the population of wild Grevy's Zebra to be as high as 20,000 animals.

In reality, in an independent survey in 1977, the USFWS had themselves estimated the population to be only 1,500 animals. Despite this, two years later, under pressure from Don Hunt and the SCI, the FWS dropped its proposal and maintained the merely 'Threatened' status of the Grevy's Zebra, allowing unlicensed trade in the animals for "zoological exhibition, enhancement or propagation for survival of the species". This prompted an outraged letter from the Minister for Wildlife and Tourism in Kenya, who pointed out that in one year alone, between 1976-77 the Grevy's population had declined from 7,000 to 2,500 in one very restricted area, the Samburu district, representing an almost two-thirds decline.

So it would appear that it was very much Don Hunt, zoos and the SCI who were in control of the demise of the Grevy's Zebra, rather than international conservation bodies or government agencies.

Here, yet again, we have the grim reaper, Don Hunt, almost four decades later, sealing the fate of any proposed reintroduction of the captive bred bongos, by almost killing off the entire herd of 18 precious animals with his gross mismanagement, proving once and for all that he really didn't know what the hell he was doing. It was his reckless, and often fatal, trapping four decades earlier, of the original wild bongos in the Aberdares - with the cooperation of Seago, Parkinson, Reed and others - which irrevocably contributed to not only their decline in that particular national park but also, very likely, across their entire range in the highlands of Kenya.

Putting a brave face on that absolute disaster, Donald Bunge of the MKWC, said that "breeding had actually occurred".

That 'breeding' was the sudden appearance of an 'unexpected' calf born two days after the bongos arrived from the USA - even though the transportation by air or sea of a pregnant bongo was illegal under international law - raising suspicions that this was a very typical Don Hunt publicity stunt, in order that his Kenyan game ranch could claim the first all-American bongo calf to be born in East Africa.

A criticism of the entire fiasco by R.D. Estes in January 2006 concluded that:

"The above report; 'Summary report on Phase 1 of the Bongo Repatriation Programme', fails to mention the fact that 12 of the original bongos repatriated to Kenya in January 2004 have since died at the Mount Kenya Game Ranch, now renamed as the Mount Kenya Wildlife Conservancy, and equally disturbing, 5 of 9 calves born at the facility failed to survive."

This report was followed by a list, finally provided by the Hunt's and the MKWC after a great deal of pressure on them, confirming that by November of 2005, 12 of the imported American captive bred bongos were indeed dead. However, to add gratuitous injury to the already absurd situation that the MKWC found themselves in, due to the complete and utter disaster they had created, they then went on to claim, in the 2011 bongo ISB, to have a healthy herd of 69 animals with a total of 54 calves successfully bred between 2004 and 2011!

Another statement from the Mount Kenya Wildlife Conservancy on the refusal of the KWS to allow their bongos to be released into the 'wild', is redolent with the reprehensible attitude of Don Hunt towards the wildlife of East Africa. The Hunts attempted to justify their request for further support from the KWS by claiming:

"that the Hunt family privately already spent over $2 million on saving and breeding bongo in order to return them to the wild of Mount Kenya as a gift to the people of Kenya."

This statement obscures that fact that Don Hunt was actually banking, in today's currency, $36 million a year by recklessly and ruthlessly exploiting Kenya's wildlife for his International Animal Exchange based at the MKWC. During the years that he was "saving and breeding bongo" as a "gift to the people of Kenya", he was actually capturing wild Eastern Mountain bongo from their last stronghold on the African continent by paying the people of Kenya a pitiful 64 US dollars for each capture permit, and then selling those precious bongos to American zoos for 100,000 US dollars per animal.

That is beyond a joke. As was Don Hunt's reassuring comment made to the organisations and people who had contributed millions of dollars and years of committed work to bring back those 18 precious bongos from the zoos of the USA and Canada as a "gift to the people of Kenya". For just after assuring the deaths, by his own negligence, of the majority of these precious captive-bred animals at his private Mount Kenya Game Ranch, renamed the 'Mount Kenya Wildlife Conservancy' to gain charitable revenue, Don Hunt told his investors that: "It went off without a hitch!"

Paul Reillo, the president, founder and project leader of the programme, the man who organized and engineered this exceptional and expensive shipment of endangered captive-bred bongos to Kenya to be released into the wild, was being very upbeat about it after paying out millions of dollars for this rare event, when he told the American press that:

"Flying them there, it's not the ending. It's the beginning', Reillo said. 'It's never really finished."

Little realising that, thanks to Don Hunt, it really was finished before it had even begun. So when the American 'Association of Zoos and Aquariums' named the Mount Kenya bongo repatriation scheme as one of the "Top Ten Wildlife Conservation Success Stories' of 2006", they were obviously completely unaware that it had, in fact, been an unmitigated disaster.

Chapter Six

Sadly, Don Hunt was, just like many other so-called 'conservationists' of the time, a vacuous, vain and arrogant exploiter of the wild animals that he was, in fact, destroying in his inglorious desire to become a mover and shaker in the brave new world order of 'captive breeding'.

The highly endangered bongo of Kenya is perhaps the most classic example yet of how 'captive breeding' simply doesn't work.

The present captive population of Eastern Mountain bongo - if they are really pure bred Eastern rather than a hybrid of the Eastern and Western bongo, which has yet to be firmly established - is estimated at circa 500 animals. This then equals, almost exactly, the population of wild, genuine Eastern Mountain bongos in the late '60s and early '70s in the Aberdare National Park, where perhaps as many as 140 animals were captured for various zoos, mostly in the USA. By 2013, the estimated wild population of bongo in the Aberdare National Park was circa only 100 animals. Scientists and geneticists involved in this still on-going bongo reintroduction programme for captive bred animals from the USA - which tragically, 16 years later, still hasn't happened - claim that a wild population of forest antelope, like the bongo, that falls below a population of 500, becomes irretrievably unstable and no longer viable due to a fatal genetic imbalance.

So it would appear that it was very likely the removal of those animals for zoological 'captive breeding' experiments, from that fragile population of 500 bongo, which actually precipitated this catastrophic decline in the intervening years.

If their intentions genuinely had been to preserve an endangered species, why spend many millions of dollars over a ten to twenty year period, capturing precious wild bongo, with its associated attrition rates, to then acclimatise them, quarantine them and transport them thousands of miles across the ocean, to be quarantined yet again before travelling to zoos in America? All, in order that perhaps one day, their offspring could repeat that traumatic process in reverse in the hopes of replenishing that now depleted wild population? What zoological organisations and trappers should have done, if their intention had genuinely been to conserve the species, is pooled their massive resources to invest those millions of dollars in direct action in the natural environment and habitat of the wild bongos. Direct action such as strictly enforced laws, specifically preventing the wild trapping of bongos for the zoological market and dedicated native officers constantly stationed in the Aberdare National Park itself, to protect the bongo and its natural environment.

Recent studies have shown that trained, intelligence-gathering, native officers prove far more efficient in controlling the poaching than do armed patrols - in one instance alone it was found that a single day of intelligence-gathering was more effective than a month of armed patrols.

Such measures taken earlier could have naturally raised the population to what would be today about 2,000 animals, ensuring a viable and extremely stable population.

However, the seductive allure of the 'mirage' of 'captive breeding' conjured up by the likes of Knowles, Aspinall, Hunt, Seago and many others involved in this bleak period of zoological history, won the day.

Thus, we are instead staring into the oblivion of extinction for the remaining wild bongo of Kenya, while a severely depleted, genetically handicapped, captive-bred herd of bongo, idly chew pasture in a fenced enclosure on Don Hunt's game ranch as refugee 'orphans' that nobody wants to adopt. Especially the people of Kenya and their Wildlife Service.

Ignorance certainly triumphed in this particular case and this is dramatically illustrated by an entry in the latest edition of the ISB for the critically endangered Eastern Mountain Bongo, where the death of a wild caught 13 year old male bongo is recorded as taking place at the Dvur Kralove zoo - mentioned in earlier chapters - in October of 2017. This record indicates that this particular bongo must have been taken from the Aberdare National Park (or perhaps from the Nairobi 'orphanage') in 2004, the same year that the American zoos and associated conservation organizations spent millions of dollars importing 18 captive-bred Eastern Mountain Bongo into Kenya, to be released into the wilds of ... the Aberdare National Park. However that animal may, in fact, have been a Western Lowland Bongo, given Don Hunt's apparent willingness to substitute the more common subspecies when it suited him. An independent assessment of the genetic status of the few remaining captive bred bongo at the MKWC - and the total world herd in captivity - appears seriously to question the origins of some of these animals:

"Genetic selection of release animals may not be optimal in the light of animals still occupying that area. There is a risk that prematurely releasing significant numbers of animals of globally well-represented lines could compromise the wild genetic profile over the long-term. There are currently information gaps relating to the **pedigree** of the current Nanyuki herd *('Nanyuki' being the ISB name for the MKWC)...*
There is currently insufficient information relating to the genetics of the Nanyuki herd to draw robust conclusions."

The vitally important word used in this report is 'pedigree' - as highlighted above - so does this mean that this international, independent committee may have entertained the idea that the Eastern Mountain Bongo had been cross-bred in captivity with the Western Lowland bongo, courtesy of Don Hunt, Seago and others, and that perhaps none of the entire world herd of captive bred animals were genuine Eastern Mountain Bongos, but rather zoo-bred hybrids? Hybrids that could, and would wreak absolute havoc on the remaining fragile population of Eastern Mountain Bongo in the Aberdare National Park. For 'pedigree' actually means the record of descent of an animal, showing it to be pure-bred or otherwise, meaning that these animals may not be pure bred, but in fact tainted blood.
This catastrophic scenario of tainted blood in captive bongo appears to be reliably confirmed by the independent vet. Jerry Haigh, writing of his Kenyan experiences with Don Hunt in the late '60s and early '70s, in his book 'Wrestling with Rhinos', where he discusses his work for Don Hunt at the Mombasa quarantine station with an impending shipment of sixty wild ungulates destined for the USA. He makes the clear distinction between the animals of East

African origin - which he tranquillises first, simply because he already has had experience with them at the MKGR - and the, to him, unfamiliar animals, arrivals from West Africa; and it is right here that he makes a vitally important statement:

"By afternoon tea-time we had gone through everything **except the West African visitors**."

Which he calls: "the most valuable and worrying animals." These, of course, were the $100,000-a-piece bongo and duiker antelope that had been flown down to Kenya from the Ivory Coast in West Africa, in Don Hunt's famous 'Flying Ark', where relatively common, inexpensive and easy to catch Western Lowland Bongo suddenly and magically became the much rarer and far more expensive Eastern Mountain Bongo. An impressive bit of 'hey presto' that made Don Hunt several million dollars but perhaps at the same time, unfortunately and irrevocably, polluted the world captive herd of some 500 animals with the tainted blood of hybridization.

Jerry Haigh's statement as to the true origins of the bongo he examined at the MQS is unequivocal; and must be taken seriously by the zoological world. Additionally, in the murky world of the modern zoo, it is claimed by many that there are presently no Western Lowland bongos in captivity.

The obvious implication being that all bongos in captivity are the much rarer, critically endangered - and vastly more expensive - Eastern Mountain bongo. However, as we have seen, in the first-hand testimony of the vet Jerry Haigh, he states quite emphatically that all seven of the bongo captured by Seago and Parkinson, seen by him at Don Hunt's Mombasa Quarantine Station, were of West African origin, meaning that they were all Western Lowland bongo and could not have been Eastern Mountain bongo. When his evidence is taken into account, plus the fact that it was this triad of animal dealers of Hunt, Seago and Parkinson who supplied the vast majority of bongos to the American and European zoo market - at least fifty known animals but possibly many, many more - then the true origins of these bongo has to be seriously questioned. It does appear that a large number of these animals may well have been Western Lowland bongo, or perhaps even worse, cross-bred hybrids between the two distinct sub-species, bred at the Mount Kenya Game Ranch.

It could very well be the case that the only genuine Eastern Mountain bongos supplied to the international zoo market at that time were the 36 bongo captured by Alan and Joan Root. The fact that between the years 1969 to 1980, the captive bongo population increased from one single zoo specimen in 1969 to over 100 animals by 1980, shows the extent of the importations by Hunt, Seago and Parkinson in those early years; and if the origins of all these bongos cannot be truly established, indicating that the vast majority of so-called Eastern Mountain bongo in captivity may be Western Lowland bongo, or hybrids of the two, it implies that the entire zoo world herd carries the contamination of 'tainted blood'.

As if that 'tainted blood' in bongos is not already bad enough - whether Eastern Mountain or Western Lowland - it assumes catastrophic proportions when it appears that the captive world herd could also carry the polluted genetic input of a totally different species of African antelope, the sitatunga. It seems some reckless and ruthless zoo directors of the early 1960s decided to crossbreed bongo with sitatunga, simply because there was a dire shortage of the iconic bongos in captivity. Van den Bergh, director of Antwerp Zoo, and Goss, director of the Cleveland Zoo in the USA, came up with a series of madcap plans to change that parlous situation to their financial advantage.

In 1960, Antwerp had the only male bongo in captivity, a

Western Lowland bongo called 'Nabeli' captured at Epulu in the Congo; and Cleveland Zoo had the only female bongo in captivity, an Eastern Mountain bongo called 'Karen' who - as we saw earlier - was found as a very young calf in the wilds of the Aberdare National Park in Kenya and hand-reared by film-maker Alan Root, eventually to be sold to Cleveland Zoo in 1960.

So the original plan was to air-freight the male Western Lowland bongo to the USA where the two bongos would mate and produce hybrid calves aplenty, to supply the incessant demand from the zoo world for highly prized bongos, even when they were hybrids. However, the strict quarantine laws of the USA appeared to be insurmountable to the Antwerp Zoo and concerns about the welfare of their male bongo made them cancel that original plan.

This initial failure was swiftly followed by Antwerp Zoo deciding to take the artificial insemination route - very popular in the zoo culture of the 1960's. The plan was to extract the sperm from the Western Lowland bongo and send it to the USA by air, in a sealed container, to inseminate the female Eastern Mountain bongo at Cleveland Zoo. This was another 'hey presto' madcap scheme that ultimately failed because the male bongo became so skittish in its reaction to the mechanics of the procedure that the operators feared for his life - immobilizing drugs were still very primitive in 1960 and often deadly - and the attempt was thus abandoned.

However, all was not lost, as the director of Antwerp Zoo, Van den Bergh, came up with the most dastardly plan yet in this 'get rich quick' bongo scheme; to place his male bongo into a herd of 12 female sitatunga - a closely related species but far more common than the extremely rare bongo - to see if the two species would successfully cross breed to produce fertile hybrids.

One can only marvel today at how these zoo directors of the 1960s got away with this bizarre and dangerous engineering of the genetic make-up of a critically endangered animal, by diluting and polluting it with the DNA of a different species, with the ramifications of such devilish tinkering, spiralling into its entire future, for ever more. Perhaps eventually contributing to the fatal decline of that species both in captivity, and even more importantly, in the wild at some future date, when these captive-bred hybrids might be introduced to the natural, wild bongo population. Just as might be going on right now with Don Hunt's few remaining captive bred bongos at the MKWC.

The incredible irresponsibility of these zoo directors of the 1960s in regard to the precious bongos under their dubious control, with their vain-glorious attempts to breed bongos even when that meant cross breeding the two distinct sub-species of bongo, is hard to comprehend but we have now caught three zoo directors from the 1960s attempting to do that very thing. Theodore Reed of the Washington National Zoo, Goss of the Cleveland Zoo and Van den Bergh of the Antwerp Zoo.

This leaves one wondering which other zoo directors of the '60s and '70s might have pursued a similarly drastic and reckless course of action to obtain or breed bongos, or any other endangered species for that matter.

To then step up that already awful process by actually manipulating two distinct species of antelope into cross breeding to produce fertile hybrids, as did Van den Bergh with the bongo and sitatunga at Antwerp Zoo, is a catastrophic intervention and betrayal of all the principles and ethics of any concept of 'wildlife conservation', producing the Frankenstein's monster that Van den Bergh glibly called his 'Bongsi'.

This still haunts us today with the discovery of the birth of a 'Bongsi' in 2012 at the Fasano Safari Park in southern Italy, despite reassurances from Antwerp Zoo that the experiment had no 'visible' effect on the captive population of bongo today. DNA is not very 'visible' at any level without an electron-microscope. The fact that hybrids are still surfacing in the zoo world 50 years later, is a reflection of the appalling legacy that these unprincipled zoo directors inflicted on the last untainted, almost extinct, Eastern Mountain Bongo.

What is evident, is that further experiments were carried out at the Antwerp Zoo using sitatunga males to fertilise the two, female bongo-sitatunga hybrid calves and this too resulted in offspring.However, the results of this awful experiment became 'lost to follow up'.

It is perhaps a sign of what John Knowles was to later call the 'darker age of zoo keeping' - in which he was very much a major investor and player - that these wayward and unethical zoologists from a bye-gone age, proudly wrote up the results of their recklessly dangerous experiments in the prestigious 1968 'International Zoo Yearbook' -Volume 8, Issue 1 – where the Curator of Mammals at Antwerp, J. Tijskens, explained that:"The purpose of such a breeding project is to obtain an animal that at least resembles the bongo antelope."

The engine had seized, the clutch had gone, the brakes no longer worked and the transmission had fallen out onto the highway, but those ruthless rogues just pumped air into the tyres as if that would propel them into the future.

Chapter Seven

Don Hunt's basic ignorance of the wild Grevy's zebra of Kenya, is perhaps best illustrated by an interview he gave to the press in the year following what the conservationists subsequently called his "successful reintroduction of the Grevy's zebra back into the wilds of Kenya". As he quite freely admits himself, that 'successful' translocation was a complete and utter disaster of an unimaginable magnitude - but predictable to anyone knowing and understanding the biology and behaviour of Grevy's zebra in the wild - resulting in the deaths of at least two thirds of those Imperials he moved from Isiolo in Kenya, to Samburu and Tsavo West in 1964 and 1977, to 'save' them from the 'brink of extinction'.

Don Hunt's statement, made to the New Scientist journal a few months after this disastrous translocation, is a masterpiece of understatement given the tragic outcome, which illustrated his cavalier attitude to the Grevy's zebra of Kenya, for he admitted:

"We really don't know what the hell we're doing!"

By his careless capture techniques of trapping random Grevy's zebra, as and when they appeared to his highly mobile teams, he was actually breaking up their delicate and fragile family groups, which, unlike most other species of zebra which maintain large herds, are almost always made up of much smaller, related groups scattered over huge areas of the Kenyan wilds. These are based on a small number of mares, usually between four and eight in number, who have known one another for many years and are not dependent on any particular stallion for protection or reproduction, but who, with their foals, will adhere to the stallion that can guarantee them the best grazing and water facilities, most vitally at foaling and shortly after, when the small group is at its most vulnerable. Once this has been achieved, the mares of the herd may then seek out another stallion for their next foals, but as a united group it is highly important to note, rather than as solitary mares.

This is what Don Hunt callously failed to take into account, and that is precisely why his questionable enterprise proved to be such a spectacular failure. He was catching individual mares from various family groups scattered across the plains and then expecting them to form a cohesive herd structure with alien mares or to mate with a totally alien stallion who had no natural grazing or water facilities to offer them for producing foals.

As random individuals taken abruptly from their carefully constructed family groups of many years standing, they were incapable of suddenly and magically creating a new herd structure in the strictly confined area in which they found themselves for three months after their capture. They were captive animals in the truest sense, and many modern zoos still today fail to take into account the lessons to be learned from this fiasco from the '60s and '70s when it comes to the successful management of a Grevy's zebra herd in captivity.

That, and a powerful lot of other very vital behavioural quirks of the rare 'Imperials'.

However, that fiasco suddenly got a lot worse for Don Hunt and his 'good intentions' when he released the Grevy's zebras back into the new wild areas he deemed suitable for such a reintroduction, where the displaced zebra were immediately attacked by the many lions that were common in Tsavo and Samburu.

These animals would have been unused to predation by

lions as, where they had been captured from in the region of Isiolo, lions were quite scarce. The net result being the immediate and terrified scattering of the surviving Grevy's zebra over such a wide area that there was absolutely no chance of those individuals ever finding each other again, resulting in the subsequent death of the vast majority of them by either starvation, dehydration or predation by lions.

Unlike certain plains zebra species which quickly reform their herds after such attacks by predators, the Grevy's zebra may take many years before it is able to reconstruct a viable breeding group based on mutual recognition and long-term familiarity. The difference between enormous plains zebra herds, with their 'weakest' members being picked off by predators, is entirely different to Grevy's avoidance of predator-ridden areas and their tiny, very familiar, trusted family groups whose members are established over a long period of personal interplay.

They probably thought they were catching isolated animals, the loss of which would have no discernible impact on the overall numbers. They really didn't have the slightest clue as to the absolute havoc they were wreaking in those fragile environments - and amongst the myriad of animals that inhabit them - that they claimed to be protecting in this totally weird 'Chipperfield's' circus of 'conservation'. This circus, which involved wrenching rare or endangered animals from the wild, to place them in zoological institutions for 'captive breeding programmes' to 'save' them from what Don Hunt called the 'brink of extinction'.

In this very regard, recent studies by researchers on the ground, into the herd and pack structures of many rare and endangered East African mammals, have produced some very surprising results which may prove that these Western cowboy animal trappers of the time actually played a pivotal role in the alarming decline of these mammals, with their reckless and somewhat random animal chases.

These new studies indicate that some of these African herd and pack animals may well operate out of very restricted small family groups, composed of a small core number, who then might come together either for predation purposes, or for protection, according to species.

As an example of this complete and utter misunderstanding of animal behaviour in relation to herds and packs, we can use the Grevy's zebra as the herd species, and the African Hunting or Painted Dog as the pack species, because despite one being a hunting predator, and the other a grazing 'prey' species, they do contrarily share many similar characteristics. Chiefly amongst these, being the ability to travel across vast expanses of arid wastelands, often hundreds of miles, in search of suitable food and water resources, which they then guard and protect with great tenacity, to ensure the successful survival of their offspring. This amazing capacity to thrive using vast expanses of habitat, where other species often struggle or die, makes both the Grevy's zebra and the Painted Dog very difficult customers for the concept of containment, whether that might be in a sprawling nature reserve in Africa, or in a paddock in Hampshire.

Both species very much follow their noses to exploit new resources, in order to establish a new community based on the minimum possible numbers that could survive such a new adventure and eventually tell about it through their offspring. It is at this crucial moment in the establishment of a new family group - ultimately vital for the success of the species - when the numbers have been stripped down to their minimum that they are at their most vulnerable to outside interference.

This is precisely the moment when the modern, Western animal catchers like Don Hunt, John Seago, Tony Parkinson, Josef Vagner and Richard Chipperfield, began ransacking these newly established herds and packs to supply the 'brave new world' of captive breeding with the 'surplus stock' that appeared to be plentiful in East Africa in the '60s and '70s, thereby completely disabling a natural system that had been in existence for millions of years. They really 'didn't know what the hell they were doing' because when these animal catchers found small herds of Grevy's that were trying to establish new territories with very often as few as five mares and one stallion, they took one or two of them out for the hungry zoos waiting to exploit them, and in doing so wiped that entire family group out of existence.

For it has been proven beyond a reasonable doubt now, that the catching of just one out of six Painted Dogs at this critical stage would inevitably lead to the disintegration of the group and subsequent deaths of the other five members of the pack.

So that means that for every Grevy's zebra that Don Hunt and the other Western 'saviours' of Africa's wildlife heritage were catching for the zoo industry, they might well have been killing as many as five others, in addition to the appalling attritions rates which we have already discussed. This could be precisely why the Grevy's zebra population collapsed from 15,000 to 1,500 during the years of Hunt's unjustifiable hunts while claiming to be 'saving' the Grevy's zebra from the brink of extinction.

Many residents of what is known as the 'Isiolo Triangle' in Kenya - where Don Hunt had caught all the Grevy's zebra to move them "for their own safety away from poachers" - brought to the attention of the 'conservationists' working on behalf of the Grevy's zebra, the fact that in the mid '60s the Grevy's were a common sight grazing by the road. However, by the mid '70s most of the zebras had disappeared - coinciding with Don Hunt's first big live capture of Grevy's. By 1976 there was not a single

Grevy's zebra visible in the entire area - coincidentally, after Don Hunt's second big capture of Grevy's Zebra. The only 'poacher' was Don Hunt himself, aided and abetted by his fellow animal trappers and dealers, such as John Seago the Godfather of Tony Parkinson and of the animal trade Mafia.

Another typically shameful and destructive example of the 'rescue' of endangered wild ungulates carried out by the 'Wildlife Capture Unit' – as they liked to be known - of Seago and Parkinson, is also worth looking at. This was the much vaunted translocation of an entire herd of roan antelope from the Tana river area of Kenya to the Shimba Hills in the late '60s and early '70s, funded by the East African Wildlife Society who were concerned that the settlement of native Kenyans in the area would somehow lead to the extermination of those very scarce roan antelope. Much publicity surrounded the so-called 'success' of this translocation operation, with large articles appearing in the EAWS magazine, and the American television network, ABC, even filmed the whole fiasco from the air.

However, no mention was made of the fact that the translocation of the roan herd had been opposed by a large number of influential game wardens, including the redoubtable Ian Parker, who apparently resigned his position as an advisor because his recommendations were ignored. Despite the so-called 'success' of Seago and Parkinson's 'rescue' operation, every member of the translocated roan herd died within a month, thereby wiping out the entire herd of some 70 individuals.

The game warden Miles Coverdale commented at the time:

"As a conservation exercise it was a failure; it was as if the act of moving the roans was all that 'conservation' needed; the fate of the animals was incidental to the publicity."

And there you have it. The actual fate of the animals was entirely incidental to their conservation. It was all on paper. It was all 'glop'. It was all about the money, as we will now see.

Chapter Eight

It has already been conclusively demonstrated just how lucrative the trade in wild caught East African ungulates was during the '60s and '70s, with the Western animal traders and dealers still employing and enjoying their close and cosy relationships with the Western post-colonial administrators. These people were still very much in office even after Kenya became independent in 1963, simply because it took so many years to replace the civil service structure and then reconstruct it again with home grown officials.

With bongos and other equally rare and endangered animals commanding sums in excess of $100,000, it is little wonder that these modern Western cowboys of the African plains suddenly found themselves involved in what was to be the 'gold rush' days of wild animal capture, where men like Hunt, Seago, Parkinson and Carr-Hartley quickly became very rich indeed. Just as long as the money was there, anything was possible and anything could be hidden from the authorities and organisations that were there to control such illegal activities. Any and all health and welfare issues could be simply ignored, even quarantine; and permits to capture such ungulates were freely and easily obtainable by anyone who had the buying power to do so.

All to feed the overpowering and urgent need of zoological collections in far off Europe and the USA to possess exotic, rare East African ungulates; a need which had millionaires like John Knowles of Marwell Zoo - strangely enough like Jimmy Chipperfield did 10 years earlier - claiming to have sold their much-cherished Rolls Royce to fund the purchase of wild caught Grevy's zebras. Which also had National Zoo directors like Theodore Reed dipping into funds to pay John Seago a deposit for even more wild caught Grevy's zebras. Even that pales into insignificance though, when we catch the President of a far-off Asian country sneaking through the dark Nairobi night with a briefcase stuffed full of $100 notes as part-payment for a clandestine deal with Tony Parkinson, the Kenyan animal dealer and god-son of the Godfather of the wild animal Mafia, John Seago. If it wasn't for the fact that this crazy, wild story is the subject of proven public record, one could easily imagine it to be entirely a work of fiction with all its bizarre ingredients; and it stands as a marvellous example of what could be done in the murky and shady world of the trade in wild-caught East African ungulates.

Ferdinand Marcos, the then incumbent President of the Philippines certainly had that buying power by the suitcase full as he paid a deposit of $25,000 to Tony Parkinson that night, with a further $75,000 to follow, payable on shipment.

In fact, Parkinson made so much money out of that deal, that upon completion he allegedly retired to the Philippines for the rest of his life.

Tony Parkinson's brief from President Marcos was quite simple, he merely wanted to take the largest slice he could of East Africa's rapidly disappearing wildlife, and then transport it thousands of miles across the ocean, to transplant it onto a remote and largely inaccessible tropical island called Calauit. There it would become - according to the President - his private 'nature reserve'. But rumours, backed up by not a little evidence, appear to indicate that he had actually created this 'nature reserve' so that he and his much-cherished son could do a spot of trophy hunting in their own back yard rather than flying all the way to East Africa. This was mirrored by the so-called 'canned' hunting ranches that proliferated all over America in the '70s and '80s, especially in the southern states of the USA, using 'surplus' stock from many respectable zoos' 'captive breeding programmes' of endangered East African ungulates.

To illustrate the desire of President Marcos of the Philippines for a few East African animal-skin rugs for his den floor in Manila, we only need to examine his wish list for that year, 1976, written out for his very own wild animal capture specialist Tony Parkinson. For it was a considerable list:

"10 Topi; 10 Gazelles; 11 Eland; 12 Bushbuck; 12 Waterbuck; 18 Impala; and 14 giraffes."

However, even that considerable list, a total of 87 animals, falls short by 15 of the actual number of 102 ungulates which we know were kept for him at a "secret location". This was, very likely, Don Hunt's animal 'orphanage' because of its proximity to the only rail link to the Kenyan seaport of Mombasa. They were kept at this "secret location" until being laboriously loaded onto the overnight train to Mombasa to be exported directly by Parkinson, without the troublesome bother of having to quarantine them for the usual sixty days in Don Hunt's Mombasa quarantine station, even though this was normally mandatory for any exotic ungulates leaving Kenya. This may have been waived on this occasion due to the 'big bucks' that were being earned by the Waterbuck and the Bushbuck. This situation leaves one with a very urgent desire to know exactly what species those unlisted 15 animals were, for they might well have been bongos or other great rarities, which could have pushed the 'big bucks' far out of the range of the Waterbuck.

The fact that the deal had the approval of the Kenyan Ministry of Tourism and Wildlife, with all the relevant permits issued for both the capture and export of these ungulates, makes one wonder what all the secrecy was about anyway? It is worth remembering though, that the Assistant Minister Kariuki at that time was Don Hunt's partner in a variety of nefarious activities involving the wildlife of Kenya. The obvious implication being that Parkinson's secrecy and the surreptitious manner in which the shipment was swiftly expedited, were based on the fact that there were perhaps other endangered animals or even destinations, involved in this highly dubious deal, that were not accounted for in the permits issued by the Kenyan government. Then, of course, the animal health and welfare issues that may have arisen because of Parkinson's blatant disregard for the quarantine regulations governing the live export of animals out of East Africa, could well have had catastrophic implications for the livestock and residents at their final destination.

Just as it did at Dvur Kralove zoo in the CCSR when, in early April 1975, amongst the hordes of unquarantined East African ungulates (3,500 of them in total had been imported by Josef Vagner) an outbreak of the dreaded foot-and-mouth disease appears to have occurred. This resulted in the complete shut-down and isolation of the zoo by armed police for a considerable time. This ultimately resulted, at the very least, in the sudden and dramatic deaths of the largest herd of giraffe outside of East Africa, as it is estimated that as many as 49 giraffes - 23 of them pregnant at that time - were shot dead by police marksmen, and their bodies incinerated to prevent further infection. The officers involved in this operation became so appalled by their task that new local hunters had to be brought in to finish the slaughter. The situation may well have been much worse than that, but information about this horrifying incident has either been destroyed or is still being concealed. As the entire zoo was shut down, the keeping staff were shut in and even the zoo's director, Joseph

Vagner, was not permitted to enter, one could conclude that many other East African ungulates died from enforced neglect or were slaughtered before the zoo could re-open for business.

It does appear that John Knowles' ambitious 'dream' to save endangered species of wildlife with 'captive breeding programmes' had already turned into a dreadful nightmare within a few years of Marwell Zoo throwing open its gates to a very impressionable but innocent audience.

President Marcos of the Philippines and John Knowles of Marwell Zoological Park were actually very similar in their ambitious endeavours with regard to endangered East African animals, both being powerful dictators over their servitors, environment and the wildlife under their management. The pair of them also decided to destroy great swathes of pristine and undisturbed natural habitat under their ownership.

In the case of President Marcos, an entire tropical island, which is still in ecological meltdown from the impact of his callous scheme; and in the case of John Knowles, the large scale destruction of an ancient oak forest and its associated fauna and flora in Hampshire, with the consequent devastating effects that inevitably had on the endemic wildlife in both cases.

Ironically, they replaced that endemic wildlife and habitat with shiploads of exotic and rare East African animals which they both professed would one day replenish East Africa's devastated fauna, meanwhile John Knowles was actively encouraging the destruction of local foxes and badgers which he considered a threat to his exhibits and Marcos was doing the same to the local equivalent on his Philippine island.

However, the net result of their efforts encouraged the proliferation of canned game ranches, rather than any measurable improvement for wild East Africa.

This was a 'return to the wild' that we as very young, very naïve and very unworldly zoo-keepers, could never have envisaged back in the heady days of the early '70s when John Knowles was constructing his 'Ark' at Marwell. This was the brave new world of animal conservation, wherein the very same animals being 'captive bred' in the Ark were to end up being shot in Texas as trophies, by big game hunters. This was the ultimate betrayal of our youthful innocence and puts John Knowles and his cronies firmly in the same league as the President of the Philippines, Ferdinand Marcos, with his private shooting range stuffed full of East African ungulates.

A three year investigation that ended in 1994 by animal welfare organisations in the USA, revealed the true horror of what Knowles had created with his 'ark' of captive breeding to 'save' endangered wildlife, as it found that some of the most highly respected zoos in America were heavily implicated in the sale of 'surplus' exotic animal stock to 'canned' hunting ranches. This insidious and secretive trade had been going on since the early '70s in the USA - with 24 prestigious zoological institutions being named as having been involved in multiple transactions with such 'canned' hunting ranches for many years. After the allegations appeared in 1994, seven of those 24 zoos ceased selling to Earl Tatum, the facilitator of this macabre arrangement. In fact, Tatum traded a total of 108 threatened or endangered animals from one famous zoo alone over a four-year period, before the disturbing revelations of this investigation closed down their cosy relationship. However, despite that self-imposed ban by those zoos, others unashamedly renewed their dubious relationship with Earl Tatum and the canned game ranches in 2010, one of them selling a total of eleven Scimitar-Horned Oryx by 2015, all of which then disappeared into the murky 'lost to follow up' swamp.

Tatum had been fined previously for selling an endangered snow leopard with falsified documents, to an unauthorised person, and also, in 1986, Tatum had been the subject of an official letter from the US Fish and Wildlife Service for selling a threatened species, a Grevy's zebra in this case, to an un-named Texan who was not authorized to receive the animal, who was probably a 'canned' hunt ranch owner. Most surprisingly of all though, is that Earl Tatum is still listed in the 2018 edition of the ISB for Grevy's zebra as a registered holder of this rare and threatened animal. But Tatum is not an isolated case, as two other registered keepers of Grevy's zebra in the latest ISB are also closely linked to the 'canned' hunting industry in the USA.

One being Larry Johnson of Safari Enterprises in Texas, the other being Chase Akin of the Harkey Ranch in San Angelo, Texas, which is today just about the most successful 'canned' shooting range and 'game ranch' in the world for captive East African and other ungulates. One of the animal welfare officers involved in the investigation commented that:

"As enablers of the 'canned' hunting industry, the zoos are as guilty as the hunters who pay to pull the trigger."

Perhaps it was Dale Tuttle, the Director of Jacksonville Zoo, who captured the true spirit at that time in the '90s when he said:

"Hunting ranches are a way to make species conservation pay for itself."

For what this zoo director was saying, is that the zoos of the world are sending the offspring of their herds of rare East African ungulates, like the Grevy's zebra, to be living targets for the 'big game hunters' on 'canned' game ranches in America. The big game hunters get a Grevy's zebra rug for their den and the captive zebras back home get a bucket of pony nuts in return for the brutal slaying of their offspring. Meanwhile, three Grevy's zebra stallions stare into their own peculiar oblivion in a sketchy Djibouti city zoo, as a claimed 'successful reintroduction' from a captive breeding programme.

And right there in that oft-repeated and totally illogical statement of Tuttle's is the tragic end-result of John Knowles' brave new world of Marwell. The 'captive breeding programmes' that caused Grevy's zebra to be practically wiped out in East Africa by their capture, plus the associated appalling attrition rates on their herds, to supply the insatiable demand for them from the zoos of the world, resulted in many of those wild-caught Grevy's - and certainly many of their offspring from these 'captive breeding programmes' - being shot in the head in Texas. Simply because 'big game hunters' liked to have a Grevy's zebra rug on the floor of their den and wealthy zoo owners like John Knowles hadn't thought through their 'captive breeding' strategy. Just as Don Hunt admitted to the press after his own dismal failure to 'reintroduce' Grevy's zebra back in 1977:

"We really don't know what the hell we're doing!"

All that is left from that 'brave new world' of Knowles' distorted and contorted vision are an awful lot of Grevy's zebra skin rugs spread out on the floor of the killer's dens; rugs that once used to be the vital skin of the living Grevy's zebras.

Zebras with names like Patricia and Simon, for they were all very much individuals rather than the revolving fairground targets that the captive breeding programmes, like Marwells, produced for Texans who couldn't scrape together an economy flight to East Africa.

So they did it on the cheap in Texas, thanks perhaps, to the offspring of Simon and Patricia, those young animals that you once gently touched with your trembling hand all those many years ago at Marwell, in the sheer awe and majesty of the magnificent 'Imperial' standing in front of you. You little realised then that those two Grevy's zebra under your loving care, had actually been relentlessly and ruthlessly run down in Kenya as young foals, perhaps after watching their mothers injured or slaughtered while trying to protect them, until they collapsed with exhaustion.

Then they had been brutally manhandled into crates by none other than Don Hunt, John Seago and Tony Parkinson, suddenly to become 'orphans' at the Nairobi 'Orphanage' on Don Hunt's 'Mount Kenya Game Park'. But Patricia and Simon were even rarer than you had previously thought, simply because a large number of the Grevy's zebra caught in the wild by Hunt and Seago did not survive for more than a year once in captivity at zoos like Marwell. Adding yet again to the already alarming attrition rates associated with taking these animals out of the wild for captive breeding programmes.

As Jimmy Chipperfield famously said back in the 1950's,

there were "far *too* many" wild animals in East Africa, and something urgently needed to be done to control them! Well, the captive breeding programmes of modern zoological gardens certainly sorted out that little problem once and for all!

It was all about the 'bucks'. Not the Waterbucks or the Bushbucks, but the 'big bucks' that they were worth to him and his International Animal Exchange when he sold them to zoos all over the planet. By 1984 the IAE was the biggest wild animal dealer in the world. Don Hunt's only motive was to make a quick 'buck' out of the Bushbuck, plain and simple. His greed generated almost 40 million US dollars in 1970, his third year of trading as the IAE. The vast majority of these wild caught animals being, of course, East African ungulates, which Don Hunt claimed he was either translocating within Kenya or exporting to "save" them from "poaching", but as Jerry Haigh, the vet, points out in his book 'Wrestling with Rhinos' the vast majority of the translocations were not due to poaching pressures on the animals but rather were necessary because of the land settlement programmes of the new and independent Kenyan government.
As Haigh and other writers also confirm, the long-standing arrangement that Hunt, Seago and Parkinson had with the Kenyan authorities, was that for every animal they translocated within Kenya, they were free to capture another for export out of the country for their own profit.

Two vitally important points need to be made in regard to this arrangement, the first being, that if these animal trappers, like Hunt, really and honourably believed that by moving the animals into new areas, they would be safe from invasive new human settlements and/or poachers, then the equivalent number of animals that they took to sell to foreign zoos would have also been safe in those areas, negating Hunt's contention that he was 'saving' them from poaching. This makes their difficult capture, lengthy quarantine at export and import ports, extremely risky and stressful transportation to those zoos, a totally unnecessary exercise that was only there to ensure a massive profit for Don Hunt's International Animal Exchange.

Second, is the fact that none of the many animal translocations carried out by this triad of animal dealers within Kenya itself, over many long years, was ever successful, resulting in most cases, as we have shown, in the loss of all of the rare animals that they had translocated to 'safety'. As we showed in the dramatic case of the Grevy's zebra, this was entirely based on the lack of knowledge and expertise on behalf of these Western animal trappers.

So it appears that the Kenyan government officials trusted Hunt and his fellow animal trappers because they, perhaps naively, believed that the men knew the wildlife situation better than they did, and assumed that their judgement of what would be a 'safe' area for translocation would be based on their 'superior' knowledge and expertise.

However, the situation appears to show that these Western 'saviours' of Kenya's wild animals didn't actually give a damn about the animals that they were translocating because the tragic outcome of all of those many translocations did not dispose them to inform the Kenyan authorities of their failure, which may have had an effect on their free permits to capture and export live animals for their own commercial benefit.

So while all of those translocated Grevy's zebras, rhinos and other ungulates quickly died in their new 'safe' areas, Don Hunt was annually banking almost 40 million US dollars.

The complete and utter insanity of this strategy to 'save' the wild animals of East Africa from African 'poachers' by relentlessly capturing them to order for zoos like Marwell, is perhaps best illustrated by yet another disgraceful episode concerning Don Hunt's true intentions towards the endangered East African ungulates that he was "saving from poachers" and "from the brink of extinction". According to Hunt, he only caught animals to order from zoos, so the process of 'translocating' animals within Kenya to 'save' them, would have begun with a firm order from some such approved institution. In the following case, concerning the fate of 21 giraffe, Hunt would have then approached the Kenyan authorities with a 'charitable offer' to move 21 giraffe out of an area that was due for resettlement at some point in the future, at no cost to the government of Kenya, apart from, of course, the free permits to capture another 21 giraffes to export for his own profit. This is exactly what he did with the Grevy's zebra and rhinos he translocated, all of which died very quickly in their new 'safe' zones, which he had selected for them. Nevertheless, he proudly reported that his shipments abroad of Grevy's zebra, rhinos and giraffe were highly successful with almost no losses at all.

Those 'almost no losses at all' are to be scrutinised shortly. In 1984 Pathe News filmed Don Hunt and his wife, Iris, on what the naïve news company thought was an honourable and noble mission of mercy, to rescue:

"Twenty-one rare reticulated giraffes that were loaded on to an air freighter at Mombasa Airport on November 18 in an effort to save them from extinction."

So on the face of it, the Pathe news story appears to show two committed conservationists in East Africa, valiantly battling to save the rapidly disappearing wildlife by catching the animals, in this case 21 rare reticulated giraffes, to save them from the 'poachers' and transporting them to the nirvana that supposedly awaited them in the captive breeding programmes of the zoos of America. All very laudable of course, and in 1984, very valuable ammunition indeed for the cause of the modern zoos and their ambitions to use captive breeding programmes as a means of 'conserving' the disappearing wildlife of the world, and in particular East Africa. However, a closer look at the cosy little Pathe news clip reveals some very disturbing facts, of which the average viewer would be, perhaps, unaware. For the clip reveals that the giraffe catchers, Don and Iris Hunt and others in the crew, are proudly wearing shirts which have emblazoned on the back, the logo 'International Animal Exchange' - their own private company that just happens to be the biggest wild animal dealership on the planet - despite the fact that Don Hunt's animal dealer licence for the IAE and the MKGR had been revoked in the 1970s by the Capture Committee. Then, as the film clip shows the giraffes entering the Mombasa Quarantine Station, there is a sign clearly visible which reads 'Mombasa Quarantine Station. Owner: International Animal Exchange.'

Just before the clip ends with the giraffes being loaded on board an aircraft bound for the USA, there is a close up of the label on one of the crates, which gives the identity and address of the present owner, and this reads 'Ferndale' which is of course the headquarters of Don Hunt's International Animal Exchange. The animals belonged to Don Hunt all along, he wasn't saving them from poachers at all, for **he** was the poacher, who was merely fulfilling pre-orders from zoos in the USA for the giraffes. As we saw earlier, Don Hunt never speculated on the live animals he hunted down, but only caught them to fulfil a specific order from a specific zoo, having 'earned' the permits to do so, by hurriedly offering to translocate 21 more Giraffe within Kenya for their own 'good'.

A little known fact in this largely misunderstood world of

the capture of exotic wild animals destined for the American zoo industry, is that early legislation enacted by the Department of Agriculture in the USA required, by law, any zoological institution planning to obtain exotic species of animals from abroad, to file a request to the Department of Agriculture for a permit to do so (10.75); and that before the issue of such a permit, the zoo applying would be visited by an authorised representative of the DOA to inspect, and then approve or disallow, the intended shipment.

An equally little known fact is that the Kenyan wildlife authorities also had what was called a 'Capture Committee' who carefully vetted each and every application for the capture of wild animals, and it was their long-standing tradition to only issue such 'live capture permits' to 'authorized animal dealers' when the animals were destined for a recognised zoological institution.

This shows that Don Hunt's orders for wild animals from zoos, would have been in the pipeline for at least a year prior to his 'charitable' offers to the authorities to translocate and 'save' such animals within Kenya; and this is confirmed by the fact that every wild caught ungulate entering quarantine in the USA was required to have the identity of their intended zoological destination tattooed on their ears prior to the quarantine period of confinement.

It was for these very reasons that Don Hunt, and other wild animal trappers and dealers from East Africa, Europe and the USA, actually bought land in the USA or Europe and opened makeshift 'pop-up' zoos on them, so that they were able to import wild caught ungulates to themselves, and then sell them to other zoos, menageries, game ranches and dealers.

Meanwhile, it is well worth tracking another shipment of wild ungulates that originated in Don Hunt's IAE-owned Mombasa Quarantine Station, destined for New York. This shipment landed all concerned in the United States District Court of New York in 1971, on charges of gross animal cruelty and negligence.

In 1969 a total of 80 East African wild caught ungulates were loaded onto the open decks of the 'New Westminster City' - under the flag of the 'States Marine Line' – at Mombasa, for a four-week sailing to New York. The cargo manifest no longer exists but the court heard evidence that the ungulates included giraffe, zebra, gazelles, dik-dik and 'others'- whose actual identity only became clear during post-mortems of animals which were found to be on board the 'New Westminster City', dead on arrival. These 'other' ungulates proved, sadly, to be very rare gerenuk, Speke's gazelle and white-tailed gnu.

During the actual voyage, eight more animals died and were thrown into the sea; one giraffe, two dik-dik and five zebras, and when quarantine staff investigated the shipment on arrival in New York, they found a further four more dead zebras in their crates along with the gerenuk, gazelles and gnus.

A further 14 animals died shortly after arrival, during the process of unloading and transfer to the quarantine station. The government veterinary surgeon who examined the dead animals, found them all in a dreadful state of emaciation, which led him to the awful conclusion that the animals had actually died of starvation and sheer physical exhaustion; a diagnosis confirmed by crew members who described the animals as "having given up the will to live". All of the animals, dead or alive, were covered in terrible abrasions all over their bodies and all had considerable damage to their limbs, including open wounds. So, out of a total of 80 animals that had left Mombasa, 26 died on route, leaving a total of 54 ungulates to survive the hardships of quarantine in New York, where it is very likely that there were even more fatalities.

This appalling shipment of precious, rare East African ungulates was a joint venture between various animal trappers and dealers based in Kenya, two of which were considered outside the jurisdiction of the United States court in New York, and could therefore not be summoned. However one of the animal trappers-come-dealers was in the USA at that time and was summoned by the court to face the charges of animal cruelty and gross negligence. This was none other than Carr-Hartley - a very close friend and associate of Don Hunt, John Seago and Tony Parkinson - who had imported 33 of the East African ungulates. Acting on his own behalf, Carr-Hartley, claimed that even a loss as high as 30% of a live animal shipment did not constitute either animal cruelty or negligence as this was **the normal attrition rate in all such shipments of wild ungulates from Kenya to the USA.** He also claimed that the United States courts had only gained successful convictions in the past on live animal shipments, where there had been a 100% loss of animals. Highly disturbing cases were cited in evidence, where entire shipments of elephants and camels had been completely lost. After further legal advice, the United States court dropped all charges against Carr-Hartley and the shipping line, making the disturbing comment that a 30% loss on such shipments of wild caught animals was to be considered "normal"!

As Don Hunt was the owner and operator of the Mombasa Quarantine Station where all 80 animals of this ill-fated shipment were quarantined for 60 days prior to shipping, it seems reasonable to suggest that he was indeed one of the other animal trappers-come-dealers involved in this deadly and deeply disturbing fiasco. This also appears to be confirmed from data in the present Grevy's zebra ISB which shows imports into the USA of Grevy's zebra by Don Hunt's IAE – recorded in the ISB as 'Ferndale' – at about the same time in late 1969 as the ill-fated voyage of the 'New Westminster City'.

The fact that most of these remaining Grevy's zebras, once released from quarantine at the Clifton facility in New York, quickly died in the zoos that had purchased them - even before Carr-Hartley's court trial in 1971 - would appear to suggest that they had also suffered the extreme trauma of that dreadful voyage, where the animals died of starvation because they either couldn't, or wouldn't eat on that 'voyage from hell'.

These were the type of men that John Knowles, and his 'respectable' Marwell Zoo traded with for wild caught animals during the late '60s and early '70s, in order to obtain the raw fodder for his 'captive breeding programmes' that were going to save East Africa's wildlife. Apparently.

For John Knowles that was to be another quite similar 'voyage from hell'.

Chapter Nine

Such wild animal shipments from hell were not at all unusual in the glory days when zoological institutions like Marwell began propagating their unreliable and deeply flawed ideology promoting captive breeding programmes as a means to preserve rare or endangered animals, while their natural habitat was being destroyed. Habitats into which they claimed that they would one day, in an undetermined future, reintroduce those rare, endangered animals. Despite the fact that the habitat was no longer viable because, by removing so many animals in the first place, they were vitally and thoughtlessly contributing to the destruction of that natural ecosystem.

These animal shipments from hell remain largely unrecorded, but the frequency of such voyages must have been extremely high, as immediately after the destructive 1969 voyage we highlighted above, the next year, Carr-Hartley was at it again in cahoots with Hunt and Seago with yet another shipment of rare East African ungulates bound for New York City. Sadly, we don't have the full manifest of the animals shipped but we do know that the precious bongos destined for the National Zoo were on board. As they were worth $100,000 each animal to the dealers upon live delivery, we can be quite sure that they would have been very well looked after indeed. Unlike in some other cases where the entire shipment was worth $100,000, so the loss of a few animals may not have been so crucial.

It should have been the history of all such shipments of wild animals from continent to continent - that the animals should be 'well looked after' - but sadly the opposite appears to be very much the case, as two examples from the more modern history of Marwell zoo will demonstrate. The first being a herd of gemsbok that John Knowles had ordered for Marwell zoo from his business associate and friend, the renowned and somewhat sinister animal dealer Franz van den Brink, who had, in turn, ordered Namibian animal trappers to obtain the then very rare gemsbok on his and Knowles' behalf. However, part of the deal was that John Knowles had to arrange the shipping-out of the herd of gemsbok from the port, Walvis Bay in Namibia, South Africa, and appoint a suitable person to take charge of the animals and look after them on the long sea voyage back to England.

For some reason known only to himself, John Knowles decided that this 'suitable person' should be a teenager who had just left school, and who had absolutely no professional experience whatsoever in the care and husbandry of exotic ungulates, or any other animals for that matter. This young boy was his son, and apparently John Knowles saw that as an adequate qualification to accompany and be responsible for, these precious animals, on what Knowles himself later called the "voyage from hell". He described this shipment in his memoirs as "part of a darker age of zoo keeping", which is a strange statement for him to make, as he was its instigator and financier.

This voyage from hell shows that he was still part of that darker age of zoo keeping, just like the institution he founded, called Marwell Zoo.

According to John Knowles, the tragedy began to unfold on the docks at Walvis Bay where the hapless, inexperienced youth found the crated herd of gemsbok already waiting for him when he arrived, ready to be loaded on board the 'Worcester Castle' bound for Liverpool.

The young man had to make the best of this situation - which Knowles claims to have been a 'fait accompli' - and get the gemsbok loaded onto the ship as quickly as possible, without even having a chance to view the animals, which John Knowles says he had instructed him to do before accepting them for onward shipment. That is according to the narrative of John Knowles, whose veracity here must be seriously questioned, as we will see.

For what John Knowles doesn't say here, is far more important than what he does say. He is very careful in his telling of the tragic tale not to mention the fact that the gemsbok were probably being shipped out of Walvis Bay in Namibia because it was one of the only two ports on the entire continent of Africa where there were appropriate quarantine facilities. Therefore, it might be the case that the herd of gemsbok could have been held in the Walvis Bay quarantine facility, rather than being simply dumped on the dock as Knowles would have it.

This in itself could cast doubts on Knowles' claim that the gemsbok had been "literally caught from the wild, crated and dispatched" to be abandoned on the dock for his young son to find upon his arrival. We could, perhaps, see this claim as a somewhat fictionalised account being used as a damage limitation exercise long after the tragic events occurred.

However, it is on the actual voyage to Liverpool that the full horror of this tragic shipment of rare ungulates is revealed, left, as they were, in the hands of a totally inexperienced youth with no training in the care of wild animals. John Knowles then discloses that all of the female gemsbok were actually pregnant - he doesn't say how many but it would appear to be at least 11 gravid gemsbok.

Apparently triggered by the stress and shock of confinement over an extended period, all of the pregnant gemsbok aborted their calves, leaving the young and inexperienced 'keeper' in a state of shock and bewilderment, and not competent to deal with the awful situation in which he found himself.

It is a miracle that any of these gemsbok survived Knowles' 'voyage from hell' and one would think that it would have been in his own interest, and more particularly in the interests of the welfare of the rare gemsbok, to have sent one of the many highly experienced and knowledgeable ungulate keepers that he employed at Marwell Zoo at that time, instead of his teenage son.

However, much worse than that, is that the actions of both Knowles, as buyer, and Van den Brink, as seller, seem to indicate their complicity in this tragic debacle, for any zoo keeper, zoo director, animal dealer or wild animal trapper would be able to identify a heavily gravid ungulate, especially of the 'Hippotraginea' subfamily as these gemsbok are, because they do not disguise their condition. The experienced animal trappers employed to catch the gemsbok would have been perfectly aware of their gravid condition.

So could it just be possible that they had the remit from John Knowles and Franz Van den Brink to actually target pregnant gemsbok in a greedy and shameless desire to 'buy one and get one free'? In the hope perhaps that when the pregnant gemsbok arrived in the United Kingdom, John Knowles could proudly announce to the zoological world that his 'captive breeding programme' for the rare gemsbok had produced calves within days of their arrival at Marwell zoo, which Knowles could then dispose of as he saw fit as they were then, of course 'captive born' animals?

Talk about shades of Don Hunt and his first all-American bongo calf born in Kenya.

What is revealing though, and probably why John Knowles presented the tragic affair as a 'fait accompli', is that the shipping of pregnant wild animals was actually illegal at that time, as an experienced ungulate keeper from Marwell Zoo would have known and would, quite rightly, have refused the shipment on those grounds. So the ever-noble

John Knowles sent an inexperienced school leaver instead, who wouldn't recognise or understand the condition of the animals under his immature control? That was perhaps his 'fait accompli'.

Recent studies on gemsbok herds in South Africa – where Namibia is located – reveal that both conception and birth coincide with the lowest temperatures and highest rainfall in the region, meaning that the gemsbok herds can synchronise their breeding cycle to benefit from the nutritional advantages of much richer pasture at both conception and parturition. This vital fact would have been very well known to the animal trappers and local hunters of the area, so they would have known whether the female gemsbok they were catching, at the behest of John Knowles, were likely to be pregnant. Of this, there can be no doubt whatsoever.

We cannot now be sure of the month in which these gemsbok were trapped, simply because of a lack of information, but the fact that they were pregnant at the time of capture is a sure indication that it was between November and April when the South African game breeders and trappers would normally avoid the capture of wild ungulates, precisely because the females were likely to be pregnant and the yearling calves far too young to endure a lengthy chase, without dying from exhaustion. They knew that the relentless pursuit of pregnant females in this season may result in the gemsbok aborting their calves. Van den Brink and John Knowles would have been aware of this risk, but were perhaps prepared to take it.

At the time that John Knowles ordered the trapping of these wild gemsbok through the somewhat dubious office of Franz Van den Brink, he would have been unaware of the fact that the circumstances he describes, the mass abortion by a herd of ungulates in quick succession, is an extremely rare occurrence, almost unrecorded, in either exotic or domestic ungulates. When it has been recorded - almost exclusively in domesticated livestock - it has been the result of an accredited infectious disease which the quarantine procedures upon arrival in the United Kingdom rules out in the case of these particular gemsbok. Today, with our improved knowledge, we are able to peer back at what Knowles called "part of a darker age of zoo keeping" - which he freely admits he was a party to - and speculate as to what perhaps took place on that ill-fated 'voyage from hell'.

John Knowles himself uses the term "aborted", which strictly means the termination of pregnancy after 'organogenesis' is complete (simply meaning that the embryo has become a foetus) but before an expelled foetus can survive. This would be a very messy and bloody business indeed, with at least eleven of these rare animals losing their calves before viable parturition; and this does appear to be the very scenario that John Knowles describes. Much less brutal and bloody would have been 'embryonic death' leading to miscarriage before the foetus was fully formed.

It is also known now that actual 'abortions' are very rare in exotic ungulates. The extremely rare event that Knowles' gemsbok experienced when they all aborted their calves 'en masse' on board the "Worcester Castle' is known today as an 'Abortive Storm' or a 'Case Cluster'. When infectious disease is ruled out – as it is in this case due to the strict United Kingdom importation rules – there can only be three possible causes for the disaster that John Knowles describes:

Firstly, the starvation of the gemsbok due to under-feeding, if their keeper didn't realise that they were pregnant and didn't know enough to increase their rations accordingly. This could have been prevented if Knowles had sent one of his many highly experienced ungulate keepers, rather than a school leaver with no experience.

Secondly, if the pregnant gemsbok had been chemically immobilized at any point in their capture, quarantine, or in the process of placing them in crates for shipment, this process could have induced abortion. This should not have happened, but it may well have done, as both Knowles and Van den Brink were very fond of the 'capture gun'.

The third scenario is perhaps the simplest and best explanation for this 'Abortive Storm', in that when you capture and relocate wild animals you actually fracture and fragment their known world, destroy their herd structure and totally dissociate them from all the familiar bits and bobs which make up their life. The massive stress of being hunted down, confined to a crate, banged up in quarantine for some weeks before and after a long and arduous sea journey in the charge of an incompetent and inexperienced 'keeper', means that abortions and/or miscarriages of such pregnant animals were only to be expected. Wild capture equals stress and stress equals abortion.

A similar but subtly different disaster took place when John Knowles placed an order with the very same Franz Van den Brink for the African ungulates which were later to become the 'signature' animals of Marwell Zoo, the highly endangered Scimitar-Horned oryx, in what John Knowles himself called "an unnecessarily bloody business". An undisclosed number of these animals were transported from Aalborg zoo to Marwell, again without any accompanying experienced keeper. Knowles blames the then director of Aalborg 'zoo' for the consequent fiasco, but 'zoo' is something of a misnomer, as Aalborg 'zoo' was really, in those days, one of animal dealer Van den Brink's many holding-zoos and quarantine stations, which facilitated his extravagant and often shady dealing in extremely rare and endangered animals.

On this occasion, it was the wild capture of 44 highly endangered Scimitar-Horned oryx in Chad in 1967 - very likely the very last herd of Scimitar-Horned oryx left in the wild - the majority of them destined for the American zoo market and 16 of them booked out to John Knowles at Marwell.

These Scimitar-Horned oryx were irrationally and stupidly placed in shipping crates that were not of a sufficient height to accommodate the long and upward-sweeping horns that give the animal its name, but slatted timber had been employed as roofing!

During the terrifying journey, the oryx's horns inevitably became trapped between those slats, resulting in the snapping off or deformation of entire sections of the horns of many of these young animals and in the case of one female, the total destruction of her entire horn structure. The result being the somewhat callous naming of some of those animals as "One Horn", "No Horns", "Crumpled Horn" and "Close Together Horns".

One can only imagine the torment and terror that these delicate and fragile, extremely rare antelope suffered in those long hours of transportation with their graceful horns trapped in the inadequate crates, a torment and terror that is well illustrated by the fact that some of the animals actually snapped off their extremely strong and normally almost indestructible horns.

These 'voyages from hell' - sponsored and financed by John Knowles of Marwell Zoo - were part of the callous tragedy of 'captive breeding' supposedly to 'save' these rare oryx from extinction in the wild.

Make no mistake, when Theodore Reed, back in 1969, talked about the 'glop' of captive breeding, he knew exactly what he was talking about. For it was, and still is, a poor excuse used by modern day zoos to justify their continued existence, in an age when those institutions themselves should have become extinct long ago. This tragic, pointless and needless shipping of wild animals around the world to fulfil the greedy desire of the zoo industry to exhibit the rarest animals left on our planet, is little reported in our modern times. The people involved in the zoo industry are not keen to advertise the massive losses of precious animals under their financial control. These highly alarming figures of the attrition rate of wild caught animals, not only during their actual capture but also in subsequent acclimatisation, transit, quarantine and transportation, remain largely concealed from the public. An audience which remains completely unaware that for every wild-caught animal that they view in the zoo, at least five wild animals may have died, if not many, many more - as we will see - in order to satisfy their curiosity and the perverse desire of zoo directors to possess the best menagerie on the block.

In 1964, when Ian Grimwood, the Chief Game Warden of Kenya at that time, was invited to address an international symposium on zoos and conservation in London, he issued a dire warning to the gathered delegates and dignitaries, acutely aware as he was, of the ever-increasing demand from zoos, on the ever-decreasing wild animals of Kenya:

"The death toll in animal capture could be huge, with many animals dying in transit."

Of course the zoo industry very politely ignored his timely warning, and the biggest 'round-up' of wild East African ungulates began in earnest that year, with thousands of extremely rare animals removed over the next twenty years to feed the voracious demands of the zoo industry and their 'glop' of captive breeding. Notwithstanding the fact that even some fifty years later the number of captive-bred ungulates in zoos, when the associated attrition rates are taken into account, has almost never matched, let alone outstripped, the decimation of the original wild herds and that to date, not a single captive bred East African ungulate has been reintroduced into the wild from where it's ancestors were taken. The best efforts of the zoos concerned, to convince the world that it is all going according to plan and that there are valid re-introduction programmes, are pure glop, which ignore the appalling attrition rates which accompany the capture and transportation of such wild ungulates.

As we have just said, there are appalling attrition rates that always apply to the capture and subsequent transportation of wild ungulates. It is entirely regrettable that, a few years later, Ian Grimwood ignored his own timely warning, when he himself was involved in a tragic endeavour, organised by the Fauna Preservation Society, to 'rescue' the last remaining Arabian Oryx in the Arabian desert wilderness. In the first attempt, two of the endangered antelope quickly died, one of them, sadly, proving to be a female in calf. Then even after a sojourn with the ever present John Seago back in Kenya, who conveniently provided the FPS with some random Beisa oryx he just happened to have on hand to practise with, the second attempt was again a tragic failure, resulting in the death of what was probably the very last surviving wild Arabian oryx. The large bull died of exhaustion after a twenty-minute vehicle chase by the FPS 'rescue' team. Even the hard-bitten Chipperfield crew of animal catchers would not pursue an ungulate for more than two minutes by vehicle, because they knew it would lead to its death from simple exhaustion, but Grimwood chased that Arabian oryx relentlessly for over ten times that crucial limit. An act that can only be described as downright reckless.

Ian Grimwood was bullish about the unnecessary death of this incredibly rare creature:

"The species appeared doomed, and the individual appeared certain to fall victim to the raiders on their next visit, it seemed justifiable to continue."

That is unquestionably 'glop'.

Later, when Ian Grimwood visited the city of Riyadh to collect two more Arabian oryx – as a gift from the King of Saudi Arabia to the world herd in Phoenix, Arizona – he was absolutely astounded to discover a breeding herd of 13 extremely healthy Arabian oryx in the king's private zoo there; thereby totally negating the need for his Indiana Jones style raids into the desert to 'rescue' the last individuals from extinction, as the King of Saudi Arabia had already 'rescued' and bred Arabian oryx many years before, without the help of either the FPS or Ian Grimwood.

This type of amateurish blundering is sadly the 'norm' when it comes to the live capture of wild animals. For us to come close to calculating the rate of attrition when taking individual animals from the wild, it is necessary for us to delve into the little history that is now known from those wild days of 'bring 'em back alive' which sadly still continue to the present day.

Perhaps the best place to start is in 1910 when the director of the Bronx Zoo in the USA, Hornaday, wrote a letter to the famous animal catcher and dealer, Hagenbeck, asking him to be 'circumspect' in his descriptions of how he obtained wild animals:
"We must keep very silent about the 40 large Indian rhinos being killed in capturing the four young ones!"

After the death of one of those four young Indian rhinos at the Bronx Zoo, Hornaday once again wrote to Hagenbeck:

"Three young captive survivors will be of more benefit to the world at large than the 40 dead ones that would have been running wild in the jungles of Nepal and seen only at rare intervals by a few ignorant natives."

And there we have it, summed up most succinctly by this zoo director; that "captive survivors" are of more "benefit to the world" than the animals "running wild in the jungles" where they are only going to be seen by "ignorant natives."!

That despicable attitude has not really changed since 1910 and is very prevalent in modern zoos, where they see animals in the wild as having no 'benefit' whatsoever, being unable to exploit them there. After all, only "ignorant natives" might see them in the wild context and habitat, whereas in their modern and splendid zoos, the captive animals will "benefit" the affluent members of an ignorant society that despite destroying their own environment and the associated wildlife, still feel that they are superior to the "ignorant natives" who actually understood and managed their own environment and wildlife much better than any Western culture or society has ever done.

Meanwhile, the total destruction of the environment and the wildlife in the lands inhabited by those "ignorant natives" has largely been engineered and carried out by a group of elitist settlers from the Western world, men just like Don Hunt, John Seago and Tony Parkinson, who at the behest of zoo directors like John Knowles, Hornaday and Theodore Reed have stripped East Africa of its scarce and spectacular herd animals, leaving behind them a trail of carnage and destruction which is still impacting on that fragile environment fifty years later. As can quite clearly be seen, there is not really a great deal of difference in the sentiments expressed, between the statement of Hornaday in 1910 and the statement of Ian Grimwood fifty years later, in that it was far more acceptable for an educated and supposedly civilised white man to kill an extremely rare animal like the Arabian oryx, to save it from being taken by an "ignorant native". This is the same justification used for the killing of 40 adult Indian rhinos in their native environment to provide 4 young rhinos for a gullible Western audience in a zoo in the United States of America.

This is the type of irrational rationale that is still being employed today in the modern zoo industry, and it is still very much the justification for the unjustifiable attrition rate that always accompanies the capture of live wild animals.

This particularly callous brutality towards wild animals appears to be a hallmark of animal dealers and traders.

In a rare disclosure, at a zoological conference in 1914, the director of Vienna Zoo, Knauer, astonished the delegates by roundly condemning Copenhagen Zoo for:

"The 28 musk oxen that had to die to provide a single young live musk ox for display purpose".

So for one calf, an entire herd of 28 protective adults were shot, as it is the musk oxen's endearing habit to form a protective and impenetrable ring around their calves which is a superb protection against wolves but mass suicide when faced by ruthless animal dealers and trappers with rifles.

The most famous animal trapper and dealer family of all time, the Hagenbecks, astounded the zoological world in the 1920's with a display of live walrus babies, a species never before seen in captivity. Hagenbeck seemed proud to discuss the method of capture and the attrition rates, despite the warning ten years earlier from the director of the Bronx Zoo not to do so:

"In order to catch the young walrus it is necessary to kill the mother. With the capture of five young walrus recently brought to Stellingen Zoo, 68 adult walruses were killed."

He then went on to explain that:

"A third to a half of all captured animals soon die from the stress of the hunt. Barely half of the animals survive the journey from the interior to the port of destination, and then two-thirds of those remaining animals die on the journey."

That statement requires some serious thought. Basically,

what Hagenbeck is saying, is that for every 13 animals he captured, only a single one would make it alive to a zoological institute and even this appalling figure does not take into account the deaths of countless adult animals – such as the Indian rhinos or the walrus, which were simply slaughtered by the trappers in order to obtain the youngsters. This means that in his first 20 years of animal trading (from the 1880's) when he sold 750 African ungulates, including 150 giraffe, plus 17 Indian rhino – amongst many other species of wild animals – to obtain those zoological exhibits would have quite possibly entailed the deaths of as many as 10,000 animals. Given the correspondence between Hagenbeck and Hornaday in 1910 where it is mentioned that 40 Indian rhinos had to be killed to obtain four calves, it would appear that as many as 170 adult Indian rhinos might have died to enable the capture of 17 calves, however the attrition rates in subsequent transportation required him to have caught at least 250 calves in order to bring home 17 alive!

So, 28 dead musk oxen in the wild equals one musk ox calf in a zoo.

Fourteen dead adults in the wild for one walrus youngster in the zoo.

One hundred and twenty dead Indian rhinos equal one calf in a zoological exhibition.

Of course, the comfortable director of the modern zoo will sit back comfortably in his comfortable leather armchair and smugly dismiss all of this as "part of a darker age of zoo keeping".

As will presently be shown though, this "darker age of zoo keeping" including massive attrition rates of wild animals, was still very much in vogue in the 1960s right through to the 1990s.

Albeit somewhat reduced by faster and more efficient transportation developments but still at a primitive and totally unacceptable level. In modern zoo keeping, supposedly in a much more enlightened age, we must now also take into account the attrition rates of surplus captive bred animals which are being sent off to 'canned' game ranches in the USA and elsewhere, to be shot by wealthy big game hunters who no longer rule the roost in East Africa.

In a later chapter the status of the Takhi - Przewalski's Wild Horse - and its relevance to conservation and captive breeding will be examined in detail, but for now it is worth looking at the early attrition rates associated with its capture for display in zoological gardens.

These are only the figures for Hagenbeck's trappers, although there were other trappers and dealers who were operating in those remote areas of Mongolia, China and Russia at the same time with similar, or perhaps even worse attrition rates:

1897 – an unspecified number of foals captured but all died.

1898 – 6 foals captured but all 6 died.

1899 – 7 foals captured, two died immediately, four more foals died soon after, and only one male foal survived the long journey to captivity.

1900 – 3 foals captured, all died.

1901-1904 – records missing, 'lost to follow up', but it was around this time that Hagenbeck somehow obtained 28 foals which he sold to wealthy gentry in Europe. These foals were captured by independent trappers who had relentlessly hunted down 25 separate 'harem' herds, shooting many of the mares, eventually capturing a total of 52 foals, but sadly 24 of these foals died on the long journey back to Europe.

1905 – 4 foals captured, three died immediately, but one foal survived.

So, in the ten long years of intensive campaigns to capture them by various trappers and dealers, an untold number of the rare and extremely vulnerable Przewalski's horses died – at least forty are recorded, but we can be sure that it was actually many, many more – to bring a few of the foals along that long road of attrition to the zoological nirvana that supposedly awaited them in the captive breeding programmes. This eventually resulted – as we will conclusively show - in them being hybridized with domestic horses to produce an animal that resembled a Takhi but was no longer a Takhi.

This is the 'glop' of Theodore Reed's and John Knowles' captive breeding survival soup, making the unacceptable acceptable and palatable to us all. The ingredients no longer exist but the taste is still there. Just as the Antwerp Zoo was proud to announce, after they had cross bred one of the rarest animals in the world, the Western Lowland bongo, with a sitatunga:

"The purpose of such a breeding project is to obtain an animal that at least resembles the bongo antelope."

Chapter Ten

In a much earlier chapter we were able to note how, as the captive population suddenly increased in the late '60s and early '70s, the wild population of Grevy's zebra decreased. This decline directly reflects the abrupt demise of the Imperial as a viable wild population, as more and more animals were captured for the sudden proliferation of zoos and safari parks in Europe and the USA.

Sadly, this highly disturbing trend can also be found in the vast majority of other rare or endangered ungulates right across Africa, such as the Sable and Roan antelope, all of the members of the oryx family, including the Scimitar-Horned oryx and addax, plus the critically endangered Eastern Mountain bongo of the Kenyan highlands.

So the removal of these rare antelope from the wild by the zoos of the world for their captive breeding programmes was very likely a major cause of the total collapse of the few remaining populations, by reducing their numbers to such a catastrophically low level that they were no longer viable breeding groups. The remaining wild populations have been spiralling into irreversible decline ever since the 1970s, when the vast majority of these antelope were removed from the wild for zoological collections just like Marwell. The example of the chaotic shipment of Scimitar-Horned oryx bound for Marwell Zoo in the ill-fitting crates which broke their magnificent horns, was featured in the last chapter. These 16 or so Scimitars were among the very last of their species to be captured in the great desert wastelands of Chad, by animal dealer Van den

Brink, to fill specific orders from zoos in Europe and the USA.   In 1967, a total of 44 animals (some records indicate 60) were captured in the remote 'Oudai Rime-Oudai Achim' area in Chad in a single expedition lasting several months. Taking into account the attrition rates associated with the capture of wild ungulates - already discussed in several chapters - it would be safe to assume that in such a remote location there were almost certainly no adequate facilities to safely house such fragile animals. As the oryx would have been captured in exactly the same manner that Ian Grimwood tragically employed in the deserts of Saudi Arabia, where he, very likely, killed off the last remaining Arabian oryx in the wild - using vehicles to run the animals down until they were exhausted enough to be lassoed - one would expect high rates of attrition. The imponderable logistics of transporting those exhausted and traumatised oryx over a thousand kilometres of largely unpaved tracks to reach the nearest seaport are bewildering, not to mention the lengthy sea voyage back to Europe.

So for every live animal that eventually arrived for quarantine at Aalborg 'zoo' it would be relatively safe to assume that at least five had died in the tragic process of capture, confinement and transportation.

Which then gives a total attrition figure of between 220 and 300 Scimitar-Horned oryx for those 44 or 60 captured for the zoological market; a figure which probably represented most of the few viable herds of Scimitars that were left in the wild in Chad at that time.

By then, the Scimitar-Horned oryx no longer existed anywhere else in the wild, so that particular zoological expedition to 'save' them, actually caused the extinction of wild Scimitar-Horned oryx. There have been sporadic and unconfirmed sightings of these oryx in Chad since then, but by the 1980's it was widely accepted that the Scimitar-Horned oryx was completely extinct in the wild. There is much irony in the zoological propaganda of 'captive breeding' as a means of preventing the ultimate extinction of a wild animal, especially when it has been the reckless and thoughtless capture of the last wild members of that species for zoological institutions, which has directly led to their ultimate extinction. The Scimitar-Horned oryx is perhaps the best icon of this irony that we have, so it is unfortunately rather fitting that Marwell Zoo - after fatally contributing to that extinction - should choose this animal as the emblem for their so-called 'conservation' programmes. The ultimate fate of those Scimitars, 'rescued' by Marwell Zoo and others, from Don Hunt's 'brink of extinction' is to be closely examined shortly.

Similarly, we can look at a scant and tiny population of Roan antelope in Kenya, isolated in the 'Ruma' National Park, which quickly reveals in microcosm their inevitable fate once the zoological institutions of the world decided to save them from extirpation in Kenya. For prior to the interests of the zoological world in captive breeding programmes for rare antelope, this isolated but quite viable population was coasting along very nicely indeed, seemingly somewhat resistant to the normal pressures of 'poaching', deforestation and loss of habitat.

But then zoo directors like John Knowles and other wealthy private individuals decided that they wanted Roan antelope for their private and commercial menageries. So they paid animal dealers like Van den Brink and Don Hunt of the IAE a great deal of money to trap those Roan, the net result being a total collapse of the wild population of Roan antelope in the Ruma National Park between 1979 and 1989, after 40% of their population was captured for 'captive-breeding programmes'! This leaves today a population of less than 50 Roan antelope in the national park; a population that is rapidly wobbling into extirpation with absolutely no hope of recovery.

That is the real, very powerful impact of the ludicrous and spurious ambitions of modern zoos to contribute to the survival of rare and endangered species by taking them out of the wild. It is a dead-end.

That dead-end of captive breeding as a supposed tool of modern conservation, is again dramatically illustrated by the bizarre revelations coming out of the then war-torn African country of Angola, concerning the only extant wild population of Giant Sable antelope in the world, located there in the twin nature reserves of 'Cangandala' and 'Luando'. It appears today, that the greatest threat to the survival of these highly endangered antelope - estimated population somewhere between 50 and 150 individuals - is the demand for them from zoos and private ranches. This demand has seen the population virtually collapse in the fifteen years since they were rediscovered there in 2005, having previously been thought to have been extinct in the wild since the early 1990s.

The subsequent population dynamics have become so insecure in the nature reserves of Angola, that a lack of adult bulls has led to the Giant Sable females breeding with the closely related Roan antelope, producing hybrids which obviously threaten the fragile genetics of their status as a distinct sub-species of Sable. It is salutary to note that when Don Hunt took out so many of the Grevy's zebra in certain areas of Kenya, the stallions that were left behind began to cross breed with the more common Plains zebra, thus making jam out of marmalade.

Such unusual behavioural inclination in wild ungulates is known today as 'The Desperation Hypothesis', where the desire to procreate with mates of the same species is suddenly over-ruled by the need to just simply breed. The zoological institutions of the world are the insidious instigators of this 'Hubb's Principle', or 'Desperation Hypothesis'.

Marwell Zoo and similar institutions did not have their

finger on the trigger of extinction. They didn't actually fire the final shot, but they stupidly loaded the ammunition into that weapon.

This lack of suitable adult males in such isolated but protected populations of rare ungulates, as in the Giant Sable and Roan antelope, appears to be strongly linked to the ambitions of both the zoological institutions and the 'game ranches' that have sprung up all over Southern Africa, and Texas in the USA. Ambitions to not only own and exhibit them, but also to breed them for commercial exploitation in trophy hunting ranches. With the current price of almost 2 million US dollars for a male sable antelope at public auction in Southern Africa, it is no wonder that this sinister cadre of well-heeled animal dealers and traders, often in the guise of 'conservationists', is beating a hasty, well-trodden and dirty path to Angola to trap these magical animals.

However, we now have to return to the iconic, and somewhat ironic, emblem of Marwell Zoological Park, the Scimitar-Horned oryx. As we have just seen, it was the indiscriminate trapping of Scimitar-Horned oryx in Chad, at the behest of zoos, that finally wiped out the last remnants of the wild population in the mid to late 1960s. Of course those zoos, and the trappers they employed, now perversely claim that it was **they** who actually saved the oryx from extinction by catching them to protect them from the 'poachers' who they avow were wiping out the animals in the uncontrolled 'wild', claiming that their strange theory of captive breeding was the only solution. This was the same excuse that Ian Grimwood employed when he killed what he knew was probably the very last wild Arabian oryx in existence: that he was 'saving' it from the 'poachers'.

So who were these mysterious 'poachers', these native bogeymen of the African deserts and savannah's, who are always offered up by zoos and wildlife organisations as the ultimate excuse for them having removed so many wild animals from the continent over the past seven decades? Native poachers are actually very thin on the ground in large and impoverished African countries like Chad, where the majority of endemic people at that time did not have the resources or wealth to mount large scale expeditions to kill wild animals for either their meat or hide, especially when they had their own flocks and herds of domesticated livestock to sustain. With their access to four-wheel-drive vehicles - essential requirements for any large scale poaching expeditions in such terrain - being almost non-existent, and severely limited by a lack of financial resources, it does seem to appear that these native 'poachers' might well be mythical creations, artfully and artificially superimposed, by the zoos and animal dealers, over the real causes of the sudden decline of the Scimitar-Horned oryx during the '60s and '70s.

The first and foremost of these heavily disguised 'native poachers' just happens to be the very zoos themselves that are perversely claiming to have saved the oryx from 'poachers'.
Their sponsorship of the animal trappers and dealers to catch these rare antelope for their menageries, probably accounted for the eventual death of at least 500 Scimitar-Horned oryx during the last known capture expeditions in the 60's, when perhaps as few as 50 animals survived the process.
However, there also appear to have been various other trapping operations carried out in Chad and elsewhere, which we still know absolutely nothing about. How else can one explain the presence of the by-now very familiar Don Hunt of the Mount Kenya Game Ranch - and owner of the International Animal Exchange - in the International Stud Book for the Scimitar-Horned oryx, as having

supplied zoos all over the world with a total of 66 animals, origins largely unknown? All of these separate transactions are listed in the ISB as having originated at 'Ferndale' which is, of course, none other than Don Hunt, the infamous 'poacher' from the already mentioned 'Affair of the Grevy's Zebra', featuring an official Kenyan government report concerning his 'shady' animal dealing in cahoots with highly placed government officials. As we saw earlier, Don Hunt was very proud to tell a press interviewer, back in the '60s, about his 'Flying Ark'; a cargo aeroplane that he employed all over the African continent to transport wild animals that he had caught. We do know that the 'Flying Ark' was used to move animals like Western Lowland bongo from Liberia and the Ivory Coast, down to Kenya and other destinations, which would have involved flying over the country of Chad, so the logistics and records do appear to suggest that Don Hunt could have been one of the early trappers of the few remaining Scimitar-Horned oryx left in the wild.

The second of these cleverly camouflaged 'native poachers' are the 'Great White Hunters' - mostly from the USA but also from Europe - who flocked to Chad in the largely unrestricted hunting days of the '60s and '70s, to bag their own personal trophies of one of their 'must have' species; the Scimitar-Horned oryx, for display in their den or study back home in Texas or Florida. We can be quite sure that the so-called 'native poachers' - if they ever existed - would not have been 'trophy' hunters, as very few of them indeed would have had the considerable skill to prepare the trophy for display in their non-existent den or study.

Numbers are unrecorded or unknown regarding this insidious trade of dead animals as trophies, but it certainly had a dramatic impact on a population that was already dwindling alarmingly because of the catastrophic effects of the third largely unmentioned 'native poacher'.

This being the gradual eradication of the fragile desert environment that supported the herds of oryx. The rapid expansion of agricultural and domestic livestock interests in the entire region, when combined with the disastrous effects of climate change, also contributed to the rapid extinction of the Scimitar-Horned oryx in the wild. However, it must be said that the resilience of wild animals to both climate change, natural and unnatural disasters, and the incursion of domestic farming and livestock is amazingly strong, and wild populations often bounce back with surprising success. The nuclear power plant disaster at Chernobyl in the Ukraine is a spectacular example of this, where wild populations of animals have not only recolonised vast areas too dangerous for people to inhabit, but have actually increased their populations to a far greater level than before the disaster occurred, once human activity was curtailed. Not however, when they are being shot at for trophies by foreign hunters, or relentlessly trapped for far-off zoological collections.

It is these last two which represent the greatest threat to any wild animal that falls onto their most-wanted list; and surprisingly that most-wanted list from both the zoos and the hunters is almost exactly the same list, for they both want the same thing, the spectacular 'trophy' animals. Basically, if the animal doesn't have a regal spread of horns, or a spectacular skin like the Grevy's zebra, then the zoos or hunters don't want them; and this premise is superbly supported by the trade in rare and endangered African ungulates today.

As an example, one can examine the past and current trade amongst zoos and hunters for three very particular and highly endangered African ungulates, these being the Eastern Mountain bongo (or even its Western Lowland sub-species), the Sable antelope (especially the Giant Sable from Angola) and the extremely rare and elusive okapi. Back in Don Hunt's heyday of the late '60s, an Eastern

Mountain bongo was worth $100,000. One hopes today that it would be impossible to buy a wild-caught specimen, but that needs to be qualified by stating that Dvur Kralove Zoo in the CCSR did that very thing in 2004. The very same year that North American zoos airlifted 18 captive-bred Eastern Mountain bongo to Kenya in a failed effort to introduce them into the wild. Despite that apparent confusion, it would be safe to assume today that a genuine wild-caught Eastern Mountain bongo would cost a zoo about three million US dollars, given that the current price of a male sable - nothing like as endangered as the Eastern Mountain bongo - would cost a zoo or game ranch almost two million US dollars.

Just as endangered as the Kenyan bongo, is the almost mythical okapi. This is a species that nobody gave credence to for many years after its discovery, as it was so unusual; but it is also a rapidly disappearing species. The okapi has since gone on to capture the imagination of a few genuine pioneers in this quirky and murky world of zoos and hunters, and has been stabilised as a wild population to the extent that they are also being managed in the wild through 'semi-captive' breeding programmes which enable this extremely endangered species to be offered to zoological collections at a price of one million US dollars per animal. They have not sold one single animal, but meanwhile sable antelope are still briskly trading at twice that price. Okapi possess only rudimentary horn-like protuberances. Sable have magnificent horns.

Now that is tragic, for it allows us to peer into the true heart of the zoos of today and see them as nothing more or less than modern day menageries. Misplaced follies of madness, insanity and confusion with no real intent, meaning or purpose.

To peer directly into the heart of the modern zoo in 2016, we can make a simple calculation based on the information supplied to us by those zoos in their International Stud Books for the two species we have discussed; the 'threatened' Grevy's zebra, and the "extinct in the wild" Scimitar-Horned oryx:

52 Scimitar-Horned oryx births in 2016.
65 Scimitar-Horned oryx deaths in 2016.
55 Grevy's zebra births in 2016.
54 Grevy's zebra deaths in 2016.

The road to nowhere.

Chapter Eleven

"A genetic bottleneck that conclusively defined the extent of the surviving gene pool occurred as a result of the capture, transfer to captivity, and variable reproduction rates of individuals removed from the wild."
(Oliver A. Ryder. Geneticist at the 'Center for Reproduction of Endangered Species', San Diego Zoo, 1994.)

Although the quote above, from Oliver Ryder, concerning the abrupt removal of the very last Przewalski's horses from the wild for captive breeding programmes, is not directly related to the present zoological world herd of Scimitar Horned Oryx, it is applicable to the fact that their entire world herd has been extracted from a few wild caught founders, causing exactly the same genetic bottleneck. This has, in turn, led to what is commonly called today 'Inbreeding Depression', a condition that Scimitar-Horned oryx are highly unlikely to ever recover from because of their small, fractured and fragmented population.
In other words, in both these cases; Przewalski's Wild Horse and the Scimitar-Horned Oryx, the capture of the last remaining wild animals for the zoological trade, has inevitably led not only to the total collapse of a viable gene pool but also virtually condemned both species to the extinction that the zoos concerned - like Marwell - were claiming to be saving them from, with their 'captive breeding programmes'.

We already saw in an earlier chapter on the Eastern Mountain bongo, that DNA samples from the much larger zoo population - circa 500 animals, proved to have far less genetic diversity than the scant remaining wild population in the Aberdares - circa 150 animals, with the wild bongo showing an incredible 90% genetic diversity in comparison to the captive-bred animals. One must keep in mind that the captive animals have spent the last sixty years in zoos scattered all over the world, and that despite an intensive management programme and careful selection of their breeding stock, the zoo animals have somehow lost the greater part of their genetic diversity. That this is the situation regarding the vast majority of endangered ungulates being held by zoos, appears to be confirmed by recent DNA research into the highly endangered Dama gazelle, with the remaining wild population of 300 gazelle having a total of 13 haplotypes, whilst the larger captive population of 550 animals having only 3 haplotypes. This is nothing less than a disaster for the ill-conceived concept of 'captive breeding', and shows it to be nothing more than a Marwellian mirage.

The brief history of the Scimitar-Horned oryx in captivity is likely to be the best example we possess of the fact that there never was a captive breeding 'programme' coordinating zoos like Marwell. As Theodore Reed, then director of the National Zoo in Washington, said in the 1960s, 'captive breeding' was pure glop to attract funding and draw people through the gate. Even in 2011, 50 years later, only 9% of all species held in captivity form a part of a co-ordinated breeding programme. That, by any standards, is lamentable.

In fact there is little evidence that their efforts to date have worked, either as a means of preserving a rare animal in aspic, or as a supposed tool of conservation, working towards the reintroduction of a rare species back into its natural environment.

It is often believed by the international zoo community, that almost all of the Scimitar-Horned oryx presently held in zoological institutions throughout the world are descendants of the circa 44 animals captured in the 1960s by the notorious Dutch animal dealer, Van den Brink in the remote deserts of Chad. There is, however, a good deal of confusion concerning this group of 'founder animals', with various sources claiming the number of Scimitars captured in Chad as being as low as 40, whilst others - like the Sahara Conservation Fund - stating that as many as 50 to 60 animals were caught. The International Studbook for Scimitar-Horned oryx itself opts for a figure of 44 animals, despite information within the studbook which conclusively shows that the total number of wild caught oryx was 63, but this figure might be confused by births in captivity soon after the animals arrived at Aalborg. Similar doubts also exist concerning the actual years of these expeditions, with 1963-1964, and 1967-1969, appearing to be the best that can be ascertained from most sources.

It is noteworthy that exactly the same confusion - about the numbers, origins and years of capture - exists concerning the critically endangered Dama Gazelle which Van den Brink removed from the wilderness of Chad at the same time as the oryx. Most claim that this happened in 1967, when a total of 35 Dama were captured in the remote 'Ouadi Hawach' region: Van den Brink himself claimed that he lost only two animals in the "harrowing" captures and subsequent lengthy transportation, eventually, to the USA. However, as Van den Brink was only able to deliver 20 Dama Gazelles to the zoos that had ordered them; 12 to San

Antonio and 8 to Catskill, it appears that a total of 15 animals died during the transportation and, or, quarantine, or were perhaps sold to private individuals in the USA. Relevant to the earlier discussions concerning the possible hybridisation of the two sub-species of bongo - the Western Lowland and Eastern Mountain - at the hands of Hunt and Seago, it is highly disturbing to note that Van den Brink also caught both of the distinct sub-species of Dama Gazelle; the eastern race and the western race; 33 of one and 4 of the other. This, once again, raises the spectre of an entire captive 'world herd' that has the tainted blood of hybridisation.

However, recent comments by those concerned in the zoo world, appear to give tacit approval to this further example of tainted blood in their captive-bred animals, as they recommend "experimental breeding" between the two sub-species to "evaluate potential negative impacts, and to see whether there is any reduction in viability of off-spring."
So, yet another chimera!

The Scimitar-Horned oryx ISB seems to imply that all the animals in zoos as of 2016 are perhaps derived solely from the 1960s Van den Brink Chad expedition. That this can hardly be the case, is conclusively demonstrated by the ISB itself, whose own records indicate that the Giza Zoo of Cairo, Egypt, has been breeding Scimitars since the late 1880's until now, and had, at the time of the Chad captures, been exchanging captive bred animals with other zoos all around the world, including Sydney, Australia, for over 70 years. In Germany alone, the Berlin Zoo took captive bred calves from Giza in 1954 and 1955. Hagenbeck's Tierpark in Stellingen took one in 1954. The calf in this case later became a parent to a male calf who lived until 1968, so was still alive at the time of the Chad capture in the early 1960s.

Similarly, as late as 1964, the Hannover Zoo of Germany took delivery of a Scimitar calf from Giza Zoo. There are also records indicating that two other German zoos were breeding Scimitars in captivity prior to the Van den Brink expeditions to Chad; a male calf, born at Cologne Zoo in 1960; and a male calf at Gelsenkirchen Zoo in 1967.

The Scimitar herd at Giza Zoo remained completely untouched by any influence from the Chad captures, the zoo having imported wild-caught Scimitars from an undisclosed region in 1949, some two decades before. The only other genetic input at Cairo was from one male Scimitar-Horned oryx from Hanover Zoo in 1966, in exchange for a female calf sent to Hanover in 1964.

This would indicate that the Cairo Zoo had sent the female oryx to Hanover Zoo in 1964 for breeding purposes and had subsequently taken the male as a result of that interchange, showing that the Giza Zoo was, even then, making concerted efforts to diversify their genetic base.

The fact that the Cairo Zoo is still breeding Scimitar-Horned oryx, in good numbers even today, shows just how sustainable their long-established herd has always been.

There were even zoos in the USA - the country that took the largest number of the Chad animals - which had been breeding Scimitars since the 1880's right through to the 1950's, like Philadelphia and Chicago, but little heed or credence is given to the genetic potential of this captive bred stock by modern zoos in their somewhat mysterious genetic calculations. For instance, no mention of a wild caught female calf Scimitar from Niger in 1968 is ever made in reference to the genetic background of the world herd; or of the three wild caught animals obtained by the Catskill Zoo of the USA in 1961, 1962 and 1963, all of which predated the Chad expeditions of the later 1960s. In addition, there is the record of a single wild caught male Scimitar, exported from the quarantine facility at Walvis

Bay, Namibia in 1976, that eventually died at Artis Zoo in the Netherlands in 1989. All these animals were already in captivity but their genetic backgrounds appear, largely, to have been sidestepped by the international zoo community and the relevant zoo authorities, in favour of taking the last wild animals from their remote stronghold in Chad and basing their 'captive breeding programme' almost exclusively on this last, closely related family. The impact of this misrepresentation and misuse of the founding members of the world herd, has catastrophic implications for their survival.

Why then, has this potential for genetic diversity been largely ignored?

This appears to be driven by some form of elitist snobbery on the part of many zoos and their errant directors, who appear to be practising a cosy 'zoological cronyism' in their tightly knit world, where nothing appears to be of importance apart from being the falsely proud possessors of the last remaining descendants of the famous wild caught Chad oryx. So instead of establishing vital data about the genetic diversity of the Scimitars already in captivity, and co-ordinating a genuine 'captive breeding programme' to maximise that home grown potential, they invested all their time, money and efforts into owning the last remaining wild Scimitars, thereby ensuring the extinction of the Scimitar-Horned oryx as a truly wild animal.

All these records indicate very strongly that the actual founder animals of the present captive zoo population encompass a much wider genetic diversity than the wild caught Chad animals, so that the assumptions presently adhered to by the majority of the breeders, in regard to diversifying the genetic background of their animals, is not only wildly inaccurate, but based almost entirely on a flawed foundation principle upon which absolutely no reliance should be placed.

The latest DNA analysis of the Scimitar world herd,

undertaken in 2020, also strongly suggested that the 'founder' population was much more diverse and larger than just the Chad oryx taken from the wild in the 1960s. It also highlighted the problem of zoos ignoring individual Scimitars because they lacked data on their historical pedigree, because many of these animals might carry a unique genetic potential of significant value in any future conservation or preservation programme for this extinct-in-the-wild species.

This short-sighted foundation principle also ignores the fact that Paris Zoo had been breeding Scimitar Horned oryx since the 1940s, with the resulting calves living at least ten years - if not longer – and being supplemented by only two animals from the Chad expedition, in 1972.

It is interesting that the animal dealer, Van den Brink, took a captive-bred male Scimitar from the Paris Zoo in 1967, the same year that he personally captured the last remnants of the virtually extinct Scimitar-Horned oryx in Chad. Unfortunately, that immensely valuable animal, perhaps unrelated to the wild caught Chad oryx, may therefore have represented a totally unique pedigree that could have contributed vital genetic material to the present world herd, which suffers considerably from a severely restricted genetic diversity. However, he swiftly became 'lost to follow up', disappearing as he did into the murky depths of the sewers of the modern zoo world.

However, it is vital to note that it was at this time that the animal dealer Van den Brink was able to exchange 'something' - all we know is that it was an animal of some kind - with the Riyadh Zoo, belonging to the King of Saudi Arabia, for two of the very last, almost priceless, Arabian oryx. This exchange incensed the Fauna Preservation Society so much that they attempted, through international and governmental agencies, to block the deal, as they wanted the two Arabian Oryx for their own 'world herd' which was then being established in Phoenix, Arizona.

Could it just be that the rulers of the Middle East had a far more realistic and pragmatic view of the parlous and perilous future of the captive Scimitar-Horned oryx held in the zoos of the world, and that they were investing their time and money into establishing a more sustainable and viable herd of captive bred Scimitars, which reflected all of the genetic diversity available to them, rather than restricting that selection of animals to the progeny of the wild caught so-called 'founder stock' from Chad?

The very awkward fact that over a twenty-year period, the increase of the captive world herd of Scimitars in zoological institutions has been a disappointingly low figure of 9.5%, strongly indicates that the captive zoo population is neither sustainable, nor viable. The latest figures from the Scimitar ISB indicate that no improvement is in sight in the foreseeable future, with 62 animals dying in 2016 whilst only 54 births were recorded. The 2004 ISB census of Scimitars recorded a total of 1,500 animals in zoological collections all over the world, but by 2016 the census was only able to record a total of 1,546 animals.

This shows that the long term - but short sighted - policy by most modern zoos concerning their captive Scimitars, is leading inexorably to yet another deadly genetic bottleneck, which may ultimately lead to the total extirpation of the scant remaining captive zoo population.
This may be a direct result of this peculiar snobbery, evidenced by the world's zoos, in appearing to rely entirely on so-called 'inbreeding coefficients' based exclusively on the Chad Scimitars as the 'founder animals' of their 'world herd'. Inbreeding coefficients which have taken as their base line, right from the very start, the assumption that the Chad oryx were all unrelated animals, a faulty and flawed premise that has since been disproven by DNA tests, which have revealed, unsurprisingly, that all of the Chad Scimitars

are very closely related indeed.

Statistics do appear to indicate that the zoological world herd of Scimitar-Horned oryx has, overall, been declining. A total of 1,500 animals were recorded in the zoos of the world in 2004, which, although the total briefly rose to 1,630 Scimitars in 2009, then decreased to only 1,546 animals by 2016. As we have already seen, even at its apex, the population of Scimitars in zoos only increased over twenty years by a pitiful 9.5%, with deaths sometimes outstripping births in some of those years. Those deaths were mostly associated with alarmingly high rates of calf mortality, which often died on the day they were born, or a few days later. This increasingly high rate of mortality in very young calves is a clear signal that the world herd is very firmly in the throes of 'Inbreeding Depression'. The high death rates in new-born animals, meaning that they die before they can become part of the reproductive potential, vastly diminishes reproductive success; thereby leading the Scimitars inevitably into the vortex of extinction.

There can be no doubt that this truly alarming situation involving the only "extinct-in-the-wild" antelope which is still extant in zoos, has been manipulated and manufactured by many of the zoos jealously guarding their 'precious' Chad bloodline, which has resulted in a potentially deadly genetic bottleneck that largely excludes oryx not derived from the Chad imports.

This, in turn, has led to many of the animals from these myopic zoological institutions, being rejected as 'genetically unfit' for any possible reintroduction scheme of the future, making the title 'captive breeding programme' something of a misnomer. The fact of the matter is - despite zoos like Marwell crowing about 'captive breeding programmes' for half a century now - that only 4% of all Scimitars form part of properly managed intensive captive breeding programmes! That means only 56 Scimitars, out of a diminishing world herd of 1,546!

In 2016 alone, 65 Scimitar-Horned oryx died in the zoos of the world, which means that more animals died in captivity than the number being actively managed in intensive breeding programmes.

That is not the road to 'nowhere'.

That is the road to perdition.

Instead, Marwell Zoo has shown, in its past, an almost shocking inability to deal with a crisis in their newly born Scimitars-Horned oryx, apparently failing to introduce suitable husbandry procedures and health measures that just might have given numerous lost calves a better chance of survival.

Since 1972, day one of their so-called 'captive breeding programme' for Scimitars, Marwell Zoo's herd has been thoroughly plagued by what is commonly called 'scouring' amongst the new-born oryx. This means a watery and continuous discharge of diarrhoea causing the death of the calf because of its inability to take up any sustenance from its mother's milk. Scouring is actually a common ailment in the calves of domestic livestock and as such, most causes are easily treated or prevented if the correct measures are implemented in the appropriate manner. This appears to be something that Marwell Zoo has perhaps not taken into account in regard to the scouring of oryx calves.

This may well be due to a false impression, on the part of the zoo and many others, of exactly what 'scouring' is in very young calves, or of its underlying causes. They instead attribute it variously to a host of largely unrelated conditions and causes, such as the introduction of a high protein, pelleted, commercial cattle diet, or the associated obesity in adults or the change in diet caused by a move from rich summer pasture to a commercial replacement winter diet.

Most of these factors appear to play no conclusive role in

the scouring of the oryx calves, apart from perhaps the abrupt change of diet, and as such, may not be significant contributory factors in this deadly scourge.

Scouring in new-borns - in domestic or wild ungulates - cannot be viewed or diagnosed as a single disease but rather, the result of several diseases, in turn fuelled by a variety of circumstances, characterised by severe and unremitting diarrhoea.

It may indeed be caused by infectious agents, most often E.coli, which then results in the inability of the calf to absorb essential fluids from the intestines, eventually leading to dehydration, which in turn causes enterotoxemia, resulting in the death of the calf from what is commonly known as 'acidosis'. Marwell Zoo often designates acidosis as the cause of death in many of their new-born oryx. However, although the acidosis is fatal, its onset and development might have been prevented by suitable management techniques which may have helped to prevent the proliferation of E. coli and the consequent death of the calf from acidosis. It is basic flaws in animal management techniques which are the major factor in any outbreak of scouring amongst calves, rather than infectious agents.

These flaws in the management of dams and their calves are mostly linked to the separation of the expectant females just before parturition, usually in special enclosed stalls that are used regularly and repeatedly for birthing purposes. This results in the crowding of mother and calf in a constrained and stressful environment, which is difficult to disinfect successfully, and risks the contamination of the calf by bacteria such as E. coli. These bacteria then proliferate in the vulnerable calf, causing enterotoxemia, resulting in its death from acidosis.

In fact, some UK cattle farmers have reported significant increases in calf mortality when they have been forced by inclement weather to bring expectant dams inside to calf, with an outside mortality rate of some 1.6% and an indoor mortality rate of 4%. This is crucially significant.

This situation is compounded by the fact that the mother's diet has been changed by her removal from pasture, to a stall, where she is fed an artificial pelleted feed. The removal of the expectant dam from rich pasture at this crucial period of her pregnancy can, and will, affect the quality and quantity of her colostrum. This substance, produced by the dam in the first feeds of the calf's life - within 2 to 4 hours after birth - will help protect it against infection, at a time when it has very low natural immunity. If her colostrum is compromised, the calf will struggle to combat any infections. At this vital moment it is essential that mother and calf are not separated or stressed even briefly, as the calf loses the ability to absorb colostrum by the hour, and could die very rapidly if separated from the mother for even a brief medical examination. So, if the mother has been exposed to a sudden change in diet and stress prior to the calf being born, there is an increased risk that the calf will quickly die due to the degraded quality of the mother's colostrum.

Unfortunately, this somewhat hasty removal of expectant dams from the main oryx herd appears to have been the 'norm' at Marwell Zoo, confining them alone in small stalls in order to give birth to and raise their calves in a totally unnatural situation, isolated as they are from the comforting structure of their all-encompassing herd. In a 2004 study by senior staff at Marwell, they actually recommended the isolation of Scimitar dams before birth took place and keeping the calf and mother together for a 'few days'. They also advised that a veterinary check and ear tagging of the calf should take place soon after birth.

However, the normal behaviour of the Scimitar dam would entail the calf lying up in cover for some three weeks while the mother joined the herd to feed, making occasional visits to the calf to check on and nurse it. By forcing mother and calf to lie together in a dirty stall all day the calf would inevitably risk feeding from her faeces-contaminated teats. This may be another contributory cause for such a large number of calves being stricken with the deadly onset of 'scouring', resulting - in many cases - in their early and untimely death from E. coli.

When confined to such a stall where cleaning regimes would have been abandoned, or restricted, in favour of not disturbing mother and calf at such a critical period, faecal matter on the bedding material in the stall could adhere to the mother or the calf, and even be ingested by the calf when feeding, thus risking overwhelming it with E. coli every time it fed.

This bacterium is, in both mother and calf, a benign and quite normal part of the gut flora, but once multiplied in faecal matter, E. coli can rapidly grow into a deadly killer of livestock, especially calves.

Sadly, at Marwell Zoo, all of these flawed procedures appear to have formed the basis of their management techniques for expectant Scimitar dams and their newly born calves, perhaps indicating why the mortality rates of newly born Scimitar calves have been so high in their collection.

Tepid measures taken by Marwell in the past to alleviate the scouring problem with newly born oryx calves have included the bottle feeding of so-called "abandoned" calves with, of all things, domestic cow's milk.

This was confirmed in 2004, by a senior member of the Marwell staff, intimately associated with the Scimitar herd, who admitted that calves had been fed with cow's milk, causing scouring. Her comments appeared to indicate that this had been taking place for some considerable time, but that recently the cow's milk had been substituted by goat's milk. Cow's milk has been known to be entirely unsuitable for wild ungulate calves since the early 1950s and is known to cause scouring in wild ungulates.

However, colostrum from domestic cows is satisfactory for

many exotic ruminants and can be stored frozen for emergencies.

In domestic livestock, 15% of all calves have a failure of 'passive transfer' of colostrum, leading to vulnerability to infections, so stored colostrum is widely used in these cases.

The regime at Marwell is therefore difficult to understand, considering that suitable milk preparations and colostrum for such ungulate calves had been available for many years, and the subject of much research and many papers in the International Zoo Yearbook.

What is truly astonishing about this revelation, is that Marwell Zoo had been in the possession of information regarding a formula for milk specifically for Scimitar-Horned oryx since the early 1980's, supplied by the Orana Park Zoo of Christchurch, New Zealand, when that zoo had the foresight to take a sample of milk from a dying oryx dam in 1981. This showed a formula with a much higher fat content than either cow's or goat's milk - almost four times as much - and also higher protein levels.

This entire sad saga may have been prevented right from the start in 1972, if Marwell Zoo had provided expectant Scimitars with a separate grass paddock, with open-sided weather shelters, where they could have been physically separated from the main herd while still having a full sensory perception of their fellow animals. Thus preventing the highly stressful, complete separation of the expectant dam from her herd. Stress, in itself, is known to have a massively depressive effect on immune responses.

The Orana Park Zoo of Christchurch, New Zealand, pioneered these successful techniques in the careful management of their own Scimitar herd back in the early 1980's and then published their results in the International Zoo Yearbook.

Do Marwell need to hold their hands up and admit, just like

Don Hunt did, that: "We really didn't know what the hell we were doing!'"?

Claims by senior staff at Marwell Zoo that "hundreds" of Scimitar calves have been bred over the last fifty years - the figure of 366 is oft-quoted - are not without reasonable foundation, as on paper, the breeding results do appear rather impressive. However these same senior staff members are not so keen to publicly discuss the mortality rates of these "hundreds" of Scimitar calves, and even the ISB - which is managed by Marwell Zoo - is somewhat cryptic in this regard, with solid and reliable information on calf mortality statistics, needing a good deal of deciphering, which even then, leaves the numbers something of a mystery.

What is certain though, is that claims on paper, to have bred "hundreds" of Scimitar calves, are not a reliable indicator of their actual breeding success. For as we already know, the mortality rate of calves has been very high at Marwell, in some years appearing to account for as many as 14 calves born in one season alone, such as in 1983 and 2004, with similarly high rates of calf mortality in 1975, 1984, and 2006. Other years appear to show no breeding at all, or at least no records of any breeding, for instance 1995, 1998, 2000, 2001, 2002, 2005, 2014 and 2015. However, this might be a misinterpretation of the somewhat cryptic statistics given by Marwell Zoo.

It must be said that Marwell is not the only zoological institution in the world with such a shocking record in the early fatalities of very young Scimitar calves, as sadly, this does appear to be very much the 'norm' in the vast majority of institutions holding breeding herds of Scimitar-Horned oryx.

As we pointed out earlier, Aarlborg Zoo of Denmark, the original importers of the so-called 'founder animals' from Chad, have lost many very young calves in quick succession over the same period as Marwell. Planckendale

Zoo of Belgium almost equalled Marwell's record of losing eleven Scimitar calves, one after the other in one season - in 2003 - and they lost nine calves in 1997.

Even Berlin Zoo appears to have been incapable of stemming the deadly flow of early death for their young Scimitar calves for many a long year.

Of course, there are exceptions to this, such as we saw earlier at the Orana Park Zoo of New Zealand, who undertook radically positive steps to eradicate the deadly menace of scouring calves in their breeding herd of Scimitars; and it does appear that it is very much the zoos from 'down under' who are leading the way out of this precarious situation, as it seems that these zoos may well have some of the most genetically diverse and robust breeding herds anywhere in the world, apart from private collections in the southern states of the USA and in the Arabian Gulf.

Chapter Twelve

It is important to stress that this is not intended as a diatribe specifically against Marwell Zoo, but rather as a robust critique of the past and present management techniques employed by the majority of zoos regarding their breeding Scimitar herds, particularly in regard to the never-ending toll of calves dying soon after they have been born. However, Marwell Zoo was, and still very much is, the 'flagship' zoo for the concept that 'captive breeding programmes' should be an integral tool in the conservation of endangered species. The zoo still attaches itself to various conservation projects scattered around the world, mostly in Africa, some of which they claim to be 're-introduction schemes' in which they, and the animals they have bred in captivity, are involved. However, a closer look at these 'reintroduction schemes' later, will demonstrate that Marwell, and other zoos, have not only failed to introduce those animals into the 'wild' but that they have also failed those same endangered species in captivity, as we highlight here, by the huge number of unnecessary deaths that have occurred on their 'watch' in the last fifty years.

When all the crowing about the number of Scimitar calves bred by Marwell Zoo and the 'success' story of captive breeding, is carefully and critically examined in the International Stud Book for Scimitar-Horned oryx - which Marwell Zoo manages and produces - the shocking failure of modern zoos to contribute in a meaningful manner to the demise of animals not only in their care but also in the wild, is profoundly emphasised. The ISB reveals that out of a total of 366 Scimitar calves successfully bred by Marwell since records began in 1972, through to 2013, 166 of those calves died within a year after birth - as we have already seen, the majority of them within a week - meaning that just over a half survived; 55%. This results in an early mortality rate of Scimitar calves running at some 45% throughout most of Marwell's fifty-year history. It is useful to compare this percentage with that of the UK's beef farming industry, where calf losses have averaged 3.57% for the last twenty years. Generally, in the beef farming industry, a loss of 10% of calves is considered to be unsustainable and a loss of 20% of calves is catastrophic. The average loss of Scimitar-Horned oryx calves in zoos is more than double that 'catastrophic' rate.

This is perhaps a reflection of the fact that zoos are financially dependent on turnover from paying guests, rather than the survival of those rare, precious calves which are largely unimportant to the immediate success of those zoos as commercial organisations.

Perhaps the past and present circumstances of the zoo world herd of Scimitars, is best reflected in a 2011 independent survey of the performance of zoological institutions worldwide, which highlighted: firstly, the maintenance of their endangered animals in a manner and condition suitable to sustain their population in captivity, and secondly, their efforts to ensure that their animals were actually robust and fit - physically as well as genetically - for any foreseeable future schemes to introduce them into their original natural habitat.

The observations and results of this survey make sober reading for the world zoo community at large and, as such, encapsulate perfectly the present parlous situation in which the world zoo herd of Scimitar-Horned oryx finds itself today.

The report importantly concluded - with particular regard to the Scimitar-Horned oryx - that the captive populations of almost all rare or endangered species presently being held by zoos, is genetically unfit and hence vulnerable to extinction; and that neither the global or regional herds of the extinct-in-the-wild Scimitar-Horned oryx being held in zoos, had any long term chance of survival because of their fragmented population of circa 1,560 animals scattered all over the world in 156 separate locations.

The conclusion reached was that the present 'zoo model' should be abandoned in favour of much larger population strategies, as present captive groups are currently not self-sustainable, simply because of their fragmented nature and isolation from each other. Urgent and rapid population growth was badly needed to maintain the genetic diversity of the Scimitar, because a larger centralised population - 500 or more animals held in one collection - retains genetic diversity with a 35% increase in numbers per annum, whilst a small herd as presently maintained by the majority of zoos will only increase at a rate of 0.35% per annum.

This restricted and fragmented population growth that we presently see in the zoos of the world, inexorably leads to the genetic defects which are the hallmark of inbreeding depression, because harmful genes are minimised in large populations but fatally maximised in small populations. The inevitable conclusion is that captive breeding programmes cannot be considered to be either viable or practical in any long-term conservation plan, unless those captive populations are permanently self-sustaining. Given the statistics from Marwell and other major zoos over a fifty-year period, this is plainly not the case. In fact, the reverse is probably true, in that so-called 'captive breeding programmes' have, in themselves, led the Scimitar into a deadly genetic bottleneck from which there appears little chance of recovery.

A useful comparison can be made between 'captive

breeding' in the zoo world of Scimitar-Horned oryx for the last forty years and Scimitar herds deliberately kept out of the hands of zoos in other parts of the world in the past twenty years.

In 2004 there were approximately 1,500 Scimitars held in captivity in zoos, representing a meagre 9.5% rate of growth in that population over forty years. A somewhat pitiful performance for what was - and still is - flaunted as a 'captive breeding programme' aiming to put those herds back into the wild in Africa. But somewhere else on this planet, other folks were less impressed with the procrastination and obfuscation of zoos with their empty rhetoric about 'conservation' and 'captive breeding' and decided to take matters into their own hands and show zoos how to breed Scimitar-Horned oryx in captivity and to introduce those animals back into the wild.

That 'somewhere' was Texas and those folks were Texans who knew how to get things done, unlike the zoos of the world.

In 2006 the Exotic Wildlife Association (EWA) of the USA - largely composed of Texan ranchers - convinced the US Fish and Wildlife Service to exempt Scimitar-Horned oryx, Addax and Dama gazelle from the Endangered Species Act so that they could freely buy, sell and otherwise trade in those three species.

Within four years, by 2010, there were over 11,000 (yes, eleven thousand) Scimitar-Horned oryx in ranches in Texas, thus increasing the world population by a staggering 400%, as compared to the paltry and highly embarrassing 9.5% increase in numbers in animals confined in zoos, over a 40 (yes, forty) year period.

This represented the greatest condemnation of the mediocre and totally inconsequential 'captive breeding programs' of zoos, who still had the gall to call their scant 1,500 animals the 'World Herd' when the Texans had just increased that

'World Herd' tenfold, in a tenth of the time that it had taken the combined powers of 156 separate zoos!

This is a damning indictment of those zoos and their performance as trustees of the diminishing wildlife of our planet, especially when one considers that by 2019 the Texan ranchers had bred a total of 15,000 Scimitar-Horned oryx! To pour salt liberally into the open wounds of those zoological institutions, the Texans did exactly the same with the two other endangered species; raising their population of Addax to a whopping 9,000 animals by 2019, and similarly increasing their Dama gazelle population to an unprecedented high of 2,500 animals. Something had gone seriously wrong for zoos here, and something had gone seriously right for the Texan ranchers.

What was that 'something'?

The most obvious candidate for the failure of zoos to step up to the mark is, and was 'glop'.

In other words what the zoos claimed to be doing on paper - in their fancy stud books, press releases and articles in the pseudo-scientific world of the International Zoo Yearbook - they were not actually doing in practice.

Just as National Zoo director Theodore Read admitted in the 1960's - all their 'captive breeding programs' and 'reintroduction schemes' were just paper trails of 'glop' designed simply to attract funding, and of course, customers through the gates of their menageries.

Perhaps the best use of 'glop' by the zoological world was exemplified by Marwell Zoo in 2015 when - with much fanfare and publicity - they opened their expensive new £3.6 million complex known as the 'Wild Explorer' to the paying public. A complex that despite its huge size, massive costs and state-of-the-art construction, actually only housed five Grevy's zebra, 11 Scimitar-Horned oryx plus two to four Rhino - which thus represents a massive investment of approximately £180,000 for each individual animal within that new complex. This is merely to exhibit these animals to the paying public, without a single penny of that vast sum being utilised for any kind of conservation action on their behalf in the wilds of Africa, where, as we know, the Grevy's zebra is today reduced to a population of perhaps just 2,200 animals, and the Scimitar-Horned oryx is now officially extinct in the wild, thanks to the depredations of the zoo world.

Shortly after the official opening of the new 'Wild Explorers', a senior financial manager from Marwell Zoo - now officially known as Marwell Wildlife - was pleased and proud to say in a press interview, that the zoo planned to invest the truly staggering sum of another £17 million sterling over the next ten years, to improve exhibits and facilities for their all-important paying public so as to "up their game" as a major local attraction. One again notes that this vast sum of money is not being spent on any form of conservation strategy or programme but purely to titillate the public who come to view these animals as exhibits in a menagerie.

Now we must take this massive sum of money into careful consideration here, especially in view of the fact that the largest ever reintroduction scheme yet to take place in the world anywhere, involving the translocation of as many as 500 Scimitar-Horned oryx from a private collection in the United Arab Emirates to the wilds of Chad, sponsored and financed by the Abu Dhabi government through their Environment Agency, the EAD, cost them US$14 million (£11,565,628) so far.

At the current exchange rate, Marwell Zoo has spent almost exactly twice as much on improving exhibits and facilities to attract paying zoo customers in Hampshire, as the Abu Dhabi government has spent on a genuine and determined conservation effort to return Scimitar-Horned oryx to the wilds of Chad, from where Marwell - as one of the zoos concerned in the tragedy - removed some of the last wild animals for their 'breeding programme'. This is a tragic farce.

The noble efforts of the late Sheikh Zayed bin Sultan Al Nahyan of the UAE to reintroduce Scimitar-Horned oryx back into the wilds of Chad has cost the EAD of Abu Dhabi circa. $28,000 per animal, whilst Marwell Zoo has instead spent the enormous sum of approximately $200,000 on each individual oryx that they reintroduced into that paddock in Hampshire where their tiny herd has been stuck for the last fifty years. So for every oryx that Marwell moved from one paddock back to the same paddock, they could instead have donated that money to the EAD and moved ten oryx from the UAE to the wilds of Chad.

Now that is a tragic waste of money and resources that should have instead been utilised for some genuine conservation work, restoring and preserving the natural habitat of the Scimitar-Horned oryx in its former range, where the efforts of private individuals are rapidly outshining Marwell and other zoological institutions, who have been claiming for years to be involved in the conservation of endangered species but have actually done very little to help them at all.

This illustrates the vast chasm between what the zoo world claims to be doing with their endless paper trail of 'glop', and what they are really doing on the ground, in the wild, to protect and preserve those rare and endangered species. That vast chasm becomes immediately obvious in the case of Marwell Zoo, where on the one hand Marwell is apparently happily utilising funds to construct massively expensive zoo exhibits at a cost in excess of £20 million, while at the same time launching an urgent appeal for charitable funds of £72 thousand to support their own failed 'reintroduction scheme' for Scimitar-Horned oryx in Tunisia - more of which later in this chapter.

The basic fact of the matter is, that it costs approximately

$16,000 a year to keep a large wild ungulate captive in a zoo; whilst it would only cost $1,000 a year to maintain that same animal and its natural habitat, in the wild. That means for every large ungulate in a zoo situation, that money could have instead protected 16 of those animals in their natural habitat.

We look here at paper trails for 'Paper Tigers'.

Marwell is by no means the only zoological institution in the world with a successful captive breeding program and subsequent reintroduction scheme for their 'Paper Tigers'; for many other zoos follow the same paper trail of 'glop' wherein they also claim to be 'conserving' rare species of ungulates but when the facts and figures are carefully scrutinised, the unpleasant truth of the matter is soon revealed: That zoological institutions worldwide have failed in the most remarkable fashion to have had any discernible impact on the fate of those rare species that they have been holding in cages for the last fifty years.

Cages that are full of promises but empty in reality, because the mammal population in zoos has declined by as much as 45% since those heady days of the '70s and '80s when 'captive breeding' and 'conservation' were first touted. This marketing hook of glop was the brand-new weapon in the arsenal of the menageries who were fast running out of reasonable or valid excuses for their continued existence, in an age when zoos were increasingly being lambasted as cruel, heartless and wasteful side-shows.

This decline in the number of animals in modern zoos has been largely fuelled by the somewhat erratic and extravagant desires of zoo directors or owners to have bigger and 'better' exhibits than their competitors, in the full knowledge that the dramatic rise in costs to finance new enclosures would mean them exhibiting far fewer animals than they had in the past. Just as happened at Marwell Zoo with their new multi-million-pound enclosure for

Scimitar-Horned oryx and Grevy's zebra, which resulted in fewer animals than they had been previously proud to exhibit in the previous, simple, but adequate, housing, paddocks and hard-standings, which had catered more for the animals themselves than to the paying public who came to view them.

Of course in the '70s and '80s, the zoos were able to increase the number of captive-bred rare ungulates, marginally, by some 5.5% but inevitably, after that initial success, the numbers of animals decreased as the population level reached its maximum potential within the severely limited space that modern zoos could offer.

This finally saw the zoo population of such ungulates decreasing rather than increasing, because the failure of Marwell and those other zoos, to implement any kind of long-term strategy to preserve, conserve or even re-introduce them, ultimately resulted in the introduction of various forms of catastrophic contraception - and even the castration or euthanasia of surplus bulls and stallions - to prevent breeding!
The zoo market was full to the brim and they did not have a clue what to do with their surplus stock, apart from selling them to Texan hunting ranches, of course, or sending them to a sketchy Djibouti zoo, claiming 're-introduction' to an area where they had never before existed.

This was never 'blue-sky thinking', particularly where the Scimitar-Horned oryx was concerned, but instead, 'pie in the sky' dogma and cant. The zoo world had done everything as back to front as they possibly could, by removing the very last Scimitar-Horned oryx from the wilds of Chad, thereby causing their extinction as a wild animal, when in fact those zoos had a substantial and sustainable population of oryx already at their disposal, in captivity. With motivated and wise management, this existing gene pool would have been more than capable of supplying the future needs of the world's zoos, as they proliferated in the '70s and '80s, without the need to remove the last precious animals from the wild at all!

The trail of destruction that these zoos have left with their management of the extinct-in-the-wild Scimitar-Horned oryx, means that between 1990 and 2008 the second most common cause of deaths in zoo oryx was euthanasia and culling!

This is the point where Marwell - and all the other zoos implicated - failed in the most spectacular manner, by causing the genetic bottleneck of extinction which still has the potential, even today, to wipe the Scimitar-Horned oryx completely off the face of our planet.

It will be remembered from earlier in this chapter that despite spending £3.5 million on a new exhibit for their Scimitar-Horned oryx in 2015, two years later Marwell Zoo was holding its cap out to benefactors for £76 thousand to finance their, rapidly failing, oryx 'reintroduction' scheme in Tunisia. This was just after putting aside a whopping £7.8 million on yet another expensive zoo exhibit, the brand new 'Energy for Life' tropical house, for which they had already received a £1.5 million grant. This is the same year that the management of Marwell was pleased to announce that they were "monitoring" and "maintaining their alertness as to the effect of the sudden drought in Northern Kenya" on the dwindling wild Grevy's zebra population, by donating a paltry £47,114 to an on-going survey of Grevy's zebra in Kenya.

It is important to note here, that much of the funding for projects like the Tunisian reintroduction scheme for the oryx and the Grevy's zebra monitoring project in Kenya, do not come directly from Marwell's own considerable charity funds but rather from organisations like the EEP (European Endangered Species Project) and their member organisations; the 'Sahara Conservation Fund', and the 'Grevy Zebra Trust' amongst many others.

This also applies in the case of the white rhino sanctuary known as the Dambari Wildlife Trust in Zimbabwe, where Marwell imply that they are still very active today in the protection and conservation of white rhinos in the 'wild', giving the impression that this is one of their many key 'survival' programmes scattered all over the world, in which they are playing a crucial role in the protection of an endangered species.

However, a closer look at the affairs of the Dambari facility quickly reveals that they are, in fact, sponsored and supported almost entirely by the US Fish and Wildlife Service to the tune of approximately £100,000 a year and that Marwell's only involvement is the payment of an annual grant – an unspecified amount of such a small nature that it doesn't appear to figure in the Dambari yearly accounts – to help cover 'core' costs. Marwell is also not mentioned in the list of funding partners but is instead classed as a 'programme partner'. Perhaps the fact that the founder of Marwell, John Knowles, helped to create the Dambari Wildlife Trust many years ago, when it was known as the Marwell Zimbabwe Trust before its collapse and restoration as the DWT, makes the modern Marwell Zoo management believe that the organisation is still being managed by the trustees at Marwell? Well it isn't and their contribution to the project appears to be negligible and all that can be reliably said is that in 2015, Marwell Zoo spent £720,000 on a new rhino exhibit. That, of course, is enough money to finance the DWT for seven years!

In 2019 much of Marwell's supposed charitable donations to its "important extension of our zoo-bred conservation" in regard to the remaining fragile Grevy's zebra population in Kenya, was actually funded by the EEP, who picked up the £20,000 tab for the ID database and monitoring equipment while Marwell itself appears to have contributed to the cost of 500 bales of hay; but the bloke on a motorbike who delivered them to the struggling Grevy's was paid by the EEP!
All of which, leaves the question begging as to exactly what do Marwell do with their own annual, hefty charity funds of circa £7 million, apart from financing their own high-tech and elaborate zoo exhibits?
It seems obvious that Marwell cannot finance such extravagant building projects from revenue raised from

their commercial ventures, because that produces, on average, between only £3 million and £3.5 million (gross) annually, most of which is already earmarked for running costs and their considerable wage bill for 305 full-time employees.
This makes it difficult to see how the zoo itself could finance extra exhibits to the considerable sum of £20 million in the last few years.

As pointed out earlier, Marwell appears to be spending the vast majority of its overall funds - both as a charity and a commercial venture - on new exhibits for its diminishing population of captive animals, rather than on direct conservation work in the field to save those species in the wild. The situation we highlighted earlier in this chapter is a classic example of where Marwell is actually investing its overall funds, as the new 2015 exhibit for Grevy's zebra cost the organisation the staggering sum of £180,000 per captive animal while in the same year they donated a total of £69,490 to 'saving' the 2,200 Grevy's still remaining in Kenya, in other words £31.50 on each wild Grevy's zebra.

This means that Marwell is only committing a mere 0.0175% of the amount it spends on one captive Grevy's zebra, on a wild one. Therefore, for every single captive animal at Marwell Zoo, that money could have assisted more than 5,700 wild Grevy's!
That alarming difference between their outlay on their own captive exhibits and what they spend helping truly wild, endangered animals perhaps shows their genuine motivations in their strangely conceived world of 'conservation'.

This ridiculous situation is reinforced by an independent report showing that out of the 1,370 endangered species included in IUCN 'Survival Plans', only a mere 1.4% of those, might, one day in the future, be reintroduced back into the wild after a 'captive breeding programme' in a zoo. That is laughable.

Marwell appears to be reluctant to discuss its funding when it comes to projects concerning their conservation activities in the wild, with their own comments on such funding being somewhat disingenuous, cryptic and obscure – for example, they talk about "fixed percentages" being set aside annually for such projects but never actually mention what that fixed percentage is. Concerning the Scimitar Horned Oryx re-introduction scheme in Tunisia, Marwell claims to be 'underwriting' the annual costs but never states what those yearly expenses are. The term 'underwriting' is so vague that it is difficult to ascertain whether this is a supportive agreement or an actual contribution of a sum of money.

They do state quite specifically that they do not give 'grants' to individuals or organisations, although, as we saw earlier, they do give an annual grant to the Dambari Wildlife Trust in Zimbabwe. Marwell also features the PhD work of numerous university students in their list of 'accomplishments' and 'projects', although, if they don't give grants to individuals, this claim seems hard to justify. In contrast, a wildlife charity - the 'Barn Owl Trust', an organisation whose accounts appear to be open, honest and transparent - devotes 86% of all its charitable funding to direct conservation work in the field, and spends less than 6% raising more funds. It appears that Marwell is perhaps doing the exact opposite of this.

Two very different worlds indeed, with the essential difference perhaps being highlighted in the small print at the very end of the document describing Marwell's charitable remit, where after the usual 'glop' about conservation and education, the following is written:

"Maintaining and developing a zoological park as a place of learning and enjoyment, and advancing the husbandry, welfare and conservation of animals."

This means that the charitable donations made to Marwell by the vast majority of well-meaning people - who probably believe their donations are going towards the conservation of animals in the wild - can be spent instead on new exhibits to attract the paying public rather than on endangered wildlife. Just as the trustees of Marwell somewhat arrogantly state in their yearly accounts:

"Funds are spent either on the zoo or charitable donations as the trustees see fit."

This then raises the question of why is Marwell asking for even more handouts to keep its Scimitar-Horned oryx 'reintroduction' scheme running in Tunisia, when it has been investing massive amounts of money into its menagerie in Hampshire for its paying public? Specifically, into the new exhibit for the remaining eleven Scimitar Horned oryx, where the trustees have 'seen fit', effectively, to spend £180,000, on each individual in their collection, resulting in the enormous sum of almost £1,980,000 on the group of eleven animals. While the oryx Marwell 're-introduced' back into the 'wild' in Tunisia cost them and their co-funders in that year, £76,000, meaning that they only spent a maximum of £345.50p on each of the circa 220 re-introduced animals. Even this minor investment is radically offset by grants and donations the zoo receives from other organisations like the Sahara Conservation Fund who, in one year alone, contributed €43,000 to the failing project in Tunisia.

Something appears to have gone horribly wrong with this 'successful reintroduction' of Scimitar-Horned oryx into the 'wild' of Tunisia. The least problem being that they have not been reintroduced into the wild at all, but are being held captive in relatively small, fenced enclosures.

Marwell Zoo freely admits that there are "No realistic prospects of Scimitar-Horned-oryx to be released from fenced areas". That applies not only to the Tunisian oryx but also to the so-called reintroduced populations of oryx in Morocco and Senegal.

The fractured and isolated Tunisian populations are being - perhaps unwisely - held in five different reserves and parks, far removed from each other, where some of the herds have seen a decline of as much as 10%: In 2017 the reintroduced oryx population at the 'Sidi Toui National Park' in the far south was suffering a 9% decline, while the animals held at the 'Oued Dkouk Nature Reserve' had declined by 10%.

The oryx in the 'Bou Hedma National Park' were devastated between the survey undertaken in 2005; when 130 Scimitar-Horned oryx were found alive and well, and 2012 when it was discovered that the population had declined to a mere fifty animals, indicating the inexplicable deaths of some eighty oryx in seven years. This was a shocking 61% decline in the largest herd in Tunisia, which still has not been satisfactorily explained by Marwell.

The only ray of hope was that the oryx being held in the 'Dghoumes National Park' had seen an 11% increase in their population by 2017. However, by 2019 that single ray of hope had been mitigated by the fact that, in the intervening two years, there had been a massive reverse and the animals there had experienced a 7% decline in their population with an associated 100% calf mortality rate.

Marwell admitted in their 2019 report, that the animals in Tunisia had been "exposed to a number of infectious diseases that could compromise the entire herd".

Perhaps this might have been prevented with better research into the conditions that the captive oryx faced when released into such a restricted environment, where additionally, hybridisation has reportedly taken place between male Scimitar-Horned oryx and female Addax, due to their unnatural proximity and the impoverished nature of the enclosures. A parlous situation which has been politely termed by some concerned, as "restricted cohabitation cause" but in reality is the result of what is now known as 'Hubb's Principle' or the 'Desperation Hypothesis', a clear indication of mismanagement and poor husbandry skills.

A desperate zoo with desperate animals and a desperate policy about exactly what to do with those desperate animals.

The 'team' from Marwell on the ground in Tunisia appeared to have little knowledge or understanding of the situation concerning the depleted herds of oryx, merely communicating their "serious concerns about the mortality rate", the causes of which still remained unknown to them.

In their 2018 report into the status of the 're-introduced' Scimitar-Horned oryx, Marwell's own 'team' in Tunisia complain about "inconsistencies in the birth and death records" and the collection of census data and then go on to make the bizarre statement that "we have found **almost** no dead adult Scimitar Horned oryx"!

However, later in the document, they express their concerns that there had been:

"an unusual number of mortalities in the adult Scimitar Horned oryx populations in 'Oued Dkouk NR' and in 'Sidi Toui NP'."

Now that is a powerful contradiction!

The only advice coming from the 'team' in Tunisia was to move the animals out of the parks and reserves and into a centralised holding facility, as there was an:

"increased risk of disease transmission from livestock, arthropod vectors and carnivores in this area."

This leaves one with the distinct impression that the term "arthropod vectors", as used by the Marwell team, has perhaps been used to obscure the fact that the Scimitar-Horned oryx had in fact been exposed to a TBI (Tick Borne Infection).

There are over a million known species of arthropods on our planet, comprising 80% of all animals, but there is only one arthropod that is likely to transmit a disease to a wild ungulate in Tunisia, and that is a tick, because we can rule out Rift Valley Fever with another arthropod vector – a mosquito – because that disease is unknown in Tunisia. When we strip away this glop, it sounds like the precious Scimitar-Horned oryx may be sharing their fenced enclosures with sheep, goats or cattle, the associated ticks which can carry deadly Theileria or Babesiosis, plus packs of village dogs, which may not only be attacking the oryx but infecting them with the equally deadly 'Echinococcus'. Indeed, independent field workers noted that one serious health issue faced by both the reintroduced oryx and addax was that the various herds appear to have been infected with 'Echinococcus granulosos', an often fatal, tapeworm infection, which is passed to ungulates from canid faecal contamination on their grazing fodder. This is also consistent with rumours that some of these oryx and addax have either been injured, or have died, from the unwanted attentions of packs of village dogs.

In addition, high calf mortality in the 'reintroduced' animals, or even, in some cases, a failure to reproduce at all, are perhaps strong indications that the animals are suffering from a TBI; a common killer of introduced zoo bred ungulates that are suddenly exposed to an unfamiliar environment and its associated parasites, to which they have no immunity. It will be remembered from a previous chapter, that it was a TBI which killed off a large number of the precious bongo antelope which were translocated from zoos in the USA to Kenya in 2004. Marwell and many other wildlife organisations should have learnt this lesson a long time ago; that animals bred in a zoo environment in another country, will have no immunity to local diseases and parasites when 'reintroduced' to a 'natural' environment in Africa or elsewhere.

When all is taken into consideration it becomes apparent that Marwell's somewhat clumsy and ill-conceived efforts to reintroduce rare ungulates into Africa have been a tragic but predictable failure.

As Marwell struggles with this disaster - appealing for more and more funds to support it, the best solution that their senior staff can come up with, in their attempt to solve the insoluble, is to create corridors that link the small, widely separated and fractured populations, so as to create, what they fancifully term, a "Meta-Population Management" programme.
That this is a totally unrealistic proposal is immediately obvious when studying a map of Tunisia, which demonstrates that the only way that Marwell could link the five quite separate parks and reserves in which the oryx are being held, separated by hundreds of miles and criss-crossed by all the major highways of the region, would be to convince the Tunisian government to turn their entire country into a national park!

Soon after this, Marwell appeared to have realised how unrealistic this preposterous proposal actually was and quickly changed their tack to physical translocations between the various parks by utilising what they fancifully call "mass capture systems".

Chapter-Thirteen

Of course, the idea of "mass capture systems" is nothing new, as the concept was pioneered by the deadly duo of Kenyan animal trappers we met in an earlier chapter, Seago and Parkinson, whose method back in the early '70s, was known as the 'Capture Unit' by the Kenyan Wildlife Service. This pair of notorious trappers had been employed to round up herds of East African ungulates in translocation schemes to "save" the animals from poaching and land encroachment. However, their results were often, if not always, catastrophic for the animals concerned, with the vast majority dying during the 'mass capture' or shortly after release. Despite this, the duo was always lauded and praised by the local and international press and authorities for their "successful" translocation projects!

In particular, their efforts to move a herd of 70 rare Roan antelope in Kenya from the Tana River to the Shimba Hills in the early '70s, was hailed as a "conservation success" story at the time. The true details of this appalling disaster were never revealed by the reporting press, for all of the animals died as a result of TBIs. The only remaining evidence of the disaster being that of the game warden, Miles Coverdale, who commented at the time:

"As a conservation exercise it was a failure; the actual fate of the animals was incidental to the publicity."

It was all on paper. Paper Tigers.

The problem here, is that almost all wild ungulates are carriers of TBIs to some extent or the other, but it is not usually life-threatening, allowing the animals to live normal and healthy lives... that is until they are subjected to extreme stress, such as pursuit and capture. Which risks transforming the harmless and common TBI into a potentially fatal disease that is more than capable of wiping out entire herds of wild ungulates.

For example, high mortality rates from TBIs in black rhinos during translocation schemes have severely limited such projects, and often ended them abruptly. Subsequent research has proved that healthy wild rhinos harboured TBI with no discernible impact or effect… that is, until they were captured, when they soon died of diseases related to those infections.

During trapping operations for the translocation of Grevy's zebra in both Kenya and Uganda in 1996, 25% of all adults died from TBIs within a week of capture and it is now widely accepted that the greatest killers are the diseases caused as consequence of a TBI when provoked and inflamed by the stress of capture or even temporary captivity. The majority of wild ungulates quickly developed deadly theileriosis or babesiosis shortly after capture. This 'worst-case scenario' of TBI is very likely to be what Marwell Zoo will be dealing with in Tunisia if they go ahead with their so-called "Meta-population management" scheme using "mass capture units" to translocate their dwindling population of Scimitar-Horned oryx from one park to another. This could easily turn into a very serious piece of 'Mega-population mismanagement' which could see many of the oryx dead in a matter of weeks, or even during the mass translocation of these animals.

The diseases caused by TBIs in captive-bred zoo ungulates are a very serious health hazard indeed, and as such do have major implications for any and all conservation programmes based on the reintroduction of zoo-bred ungulates. Having never been exposed to the natural parasites of their new environment, the animals will, of course, have no immunity whatsoever, and thus the subsequent 'reintroduction' risks being a disaster. Although we cannot be sure that this has actually taken place in Tunisia with Marwell's Scimitar-Horned oryx reintroduction scheme, it would be unusual if the animals had not been exposed to TBIs. However, we can be fairly certain that if the oryx are subjected to even more translocations using the 'mass capture' technique, the associated stress may trigger them to succumb to a TBI related disease, dying shortly afterwards.

From their own history, Marwell should be acutely aware of the risks of subjecting zoo-bred animals to TBIs in the wilds of Africa, as in 2003 the zoo introduced a number of Roan antelope into fenced enclosures in 'Mlilwane Private Game Reserve' in the kingdom of Swaziland. A further 5 Roan antelope arrived via Marwell in 2004, which were then supplemented with 3 more Roan from Marwell Zoo's old trading partner in the CCSR, the Dvur Kralove Zoo. Further information on the early days of this venture is scant and hard to come by, but it appears that from the onset, the 'reintroduction' scheme and its antelope suffered from what was described at the time as an 'unknown' disease but which was later diagnosed as 'East Coast Fever', which is one of the diseases caused by TBIs. Quite why it took so many years - and deaths, as reports suggest very high levels of calf mortality - before the disease was identified, is something of a mystery, as TBIs had first been encountered in Roan antelope in Africa in 1912, and the South Africans had been successfully dealing with the problem in their own translocated breeding herds of Roan since 1974.

It appears that in 2019, sixteen long years later, the remaining herd of Roan in 'Mlilwane' were still in the process of being moved to their final destination; another fenced enclosure on the private 'Red Tiger Ranch'. It is cautionary to remember that even today, despite very successful breeding herds of Roan being established in South Africa, any attempts to reintroduce those animals back into the wild have resulted in failure because of high mortality, particularly of calves, due to dreaded and deadly TBIs.

In 2018, a long-term 'population viability' study was conducted of a remnant and isolated population of Roan antelope which had been marooned in the remote Ruma National Park in Kenya. The conclusion was that such an isolated population of less than 50 individual antelope was no longer viable; and that they would inevitably become extinct within 100 years and would reach an irreversible decline towards that extinction within 32 years. The study also concluded that restocking the herd by reintroductions "did not show any improvement in the population growth rate"; and even more importantly that intervention measures such as restocking, provision of water sources and increased management were a "waste of time, effort and money". The number of animals in the population had already fallen too low, simply due to the trapping of the animals for the zoological market.

Obviously, this could also apply to the fragmented and isolated small herds of Scimitar-Horned oryx scattered all over Tunisia, estimated somewhat vaguely by Marwell Zoo as five herds comprising some 40 to 80 animals in each herd. It does seem that the high-end estimate of 80 oryx in each herd is rather optimistic, as this would give an overall population of some 400 oryx in Tunisia, when we know that Marwell Zoo estimates the present population at a maximum of 220 animals.

Given the confusion from Marwell's own "team", it is virtually impossible to make a reliable population estimate, so perhaps the figure of 40 animals per park or reserve is more realistic.

Taking this figure, we can then speculate that Marwell Zoo is caught here between the devil and the deep blue sea, as their five fragmented and isolated populations of around 40 oryx all appear to be in exactly the same fragile and vulnerable situation as the Roan antelope in the Ruma National Park of Kenya, having already crossed the precarious population level of irreversible decline to extinction, with perhaps, that final event only as little as twenty years in front of them. This, of course, means that the best chance of survival for the failing and ailing herds would be to move them, as quickly as possible, to create **one** large, potentially viable, sustainable herd of oryx in **one** truly safe, secure location.

The costs of such a venture would be enormous and Marwell has already asked the EEP for a £10,000 grant towards the purchase of a "mass capture system" that they intend to employ to secure and move the oryx. It is the cost of the potentially high mortality of the Scimitar-Horned oryx thus captured and translocated, that might prove to be the highest price that Marwell - and their numerous sponsors - have to pay for this somewhat paradoxical and nonsensical adventure, as it seems highly likely that the disparate oryx herds have already been infected by TBIs.

These infections will remain virtually harmless providing, of course, that the animals are not subjected to further pursuit, capture and lengthy translocations by road in the sweltering conditions common to Tunisia.

Those TBIs could then quickly develop into fatal diseases when the animals are exposed to those high levels of stress, which could potentially wipe out between 25% and 100% of all the animals concerned in Marwell's "meta-population management" strategy.

The question that simply must be asked of Marwell Zoo and their legions of experts and supporters, in regard to the 'reintroduction' of the Scimitar-Horned oryx into Tunisia, is why the devil in the deep blue sea did they not simply do that in the first place?

Why did they not place all of the 200 precious oryx – gathered from zoos all over the world - into one safe and secure location where their substantial numbers would have given the herd the viability and sustainability to truly prosper and survive?

Even their own professional staff have written reports highlighting the extreme dangers of isolating small populations of oryx, where fragmentation equals extinction, because the small and isolated herds of reduced genetic diversity leads to the inevitability of inbreeding, quickly followed by 'inbreeding depression'.

Marwell's most senior specialist in the Scimitar-Horned oryx commented many years ago that:

"Genetic diversity is retained in larger populations. A population of 50 animals is very short term. A population of 500 animals is a long-term benefit to evolutionary potential."

Perhaps they should have listened to their own highly paid specialist?

Marwell's abject failure to successfully reintroduce

Scimitar-Horned oryx into Tunisia is somewhat confused by their vague and inconclusive reporting on the parlous affair there, confounded by the fact that important responsibilities in the project, such as funding, management, husbandry, research, census and monitoring are often obscured by the sheer number of different organisations, all seeming to claim such responsibilities as their own.

A bewildering situation that is so murky and impenetrable that it is almost impossible to apportion blame or praise, or any other kind of responsibility, to any of the parties who are involved, apart from the organisation that appears to be in charge of the project and is actually overseeing it, Marwell Zoo. This, however, does appear to be the case with many of the projects that Marwell involves itself with, most notably with their two 'flagship' projects, the Tunisian Scimitar-Horned oryx 'reintroduction' attempt and their much vaunted Grevy's zebra project in Kenya.

It is particularly in Kenya that we seem to find a legion of organisations - at least twelve including Marwell Zoo - claiming that it has been "their" efforts and funds which have led to the "successful" conservation of the Grevy's zebra in the wild. However, it is not merely the plethora of organisations claiming this "success story" as their own that is confusing and deeply disturbing but the fact that these disparate organisations do not appear to have achieved any degree of "success" at all where the actual conservation of the Grevy's zebra is concerned. Instead, they have concentrated their efforts on funding fancy and expensive social gatherings - such as "white and black" themed fancy-dress balls - to showcase their glossy new reports, programmes, and ten-year plans to photo-identify each and every Grevy's zebra in Kenya. This is a process that seems to get easier every year, as the actual number of zebras to be photographed and identified is fewer every year, because they are actually not doing anything at all to save those Imperials from extinction but rather just recording that inevitable event and then slapping themselves on the back for doing so.

This is not conservation. Producing glossy coloured brochures and reports, organising symposiums, creating photo-shoots of colourful local people and four-wheel drive vehicles with 'Marwell Wildlife' stickers plastered all over the doors and having endless and expensive meetings to discuss new proposals and ten-year plans, is not conservation. It is glop.

It is widely acknowledged by this plethora of organisations, that the Grevy's zebra population is still very much under threat wherever it occurs, particularly in the south of Kenya, where it is apparently under pressure by land encroachment and poaching, causing the somewhat dislocated herds to move northwards through a narrow corridor.

Here it appears that they are even more exposed to a variety of threats and pressures, about which these organisations do almost nothing, apart from taking photos of them, counting them and making plans about how they are going to save the animals in the next ten-years.

This is what they call 'successful conservation', although, as former game keeper Miles Coverdale pointed out earlier, "the fate of the actual animals was immaterial to the publicity". In other words, the result is unimportant, just as long as the funders see some kind of effort being made. So it all looks good on the paper trail of glop, as the Grevy's zebra disappears into the waste bin of extinction while the zoos and conservationists parade their Paper Tigers for us.

The bald fact of the matter is that the Grevy's zebra population is only marginally better off today at circa 2,200 animals, than it was over forty-years ago in 1977, when the United States Fish and Wildlife Service attempted to upgrade the vulnerability status of the Grevy's, from 'Threatened' to 'Endangered', due to the alarming data the US government agency had received from a variety of sources, including one from the Kenyan Minister for Wildlife and Tourism. This material appeared to indicate that the Grevy's population had declined rapidly from circa 15,000 animals in the early '70s to a mere 1,500 animals by 1977. The letter from the Kenyan Minister confirmed the US F&W'S worst fears that the population had seen a total collapse, as he pointed out that in the Samburu district, in one year alone (76-77), the Grevy's population had suddenly declined from 7,000 animals to only 2,500. We have to remember that these are the very same years that the Western trappers of Kenya, like Hunt, Seago and Parkinson, were intensively catching Grevy's for the burgeoning zoo market of the time, Marwell being one of them. As we saw, it was their brutal and reckless trapping techniques that resulted in an attrition rate of somewhere between 5 and 10 dead animals for every live animal that arrived at a zoo.

Of course, when the US Fish &Wildlife Service attempted to upgrade the status of the Grevy's Zebra, there were howls of protests from the vested interests including the zoos, trappers, animal dealers and last, but by no means least, the powerful and influential International Safari Club. All claimed, falsely, that the Grevy's population was a staggering 20,000 animals in 1977, and despite solid evidence that contradicted that figure, the US F&WS decided not to upgrade the Grevy's status to 'Endangered' but to maintain them as merely 'Threatened', thus allowing those vested interests to continue in the unlicensed trade of the animal for "zoological exhibition, enhancement or propagation for the survival of the species".

That unwise decision was the first official sanctioning of the imminent destruction of the Grevy's zebra as a wild animal in Africa. So some 40 years ago, when 'captive breeding programmes' started to become all the rage, the wild population of Grevy's in Kenya was somewhere between 1,500 and 2,500 animals; and today it is estimated at about 2,200.

That is not a "conservation success story". That is glop.

Serious doubts appear to be cast on Marwell's own estimates concerning the present population of Kenya's Grevy's zebra, by their own comments, made in 2018, relating to 'their' census. In their report that year, about their "conservation" work in Kenya, they claim to have "found" large numbers of adult Grevy's in what they call their 'Great Grevy's Zebra Rally' - in other words, a census - which they had somehow missed in a previous rally in 2016, so, in an impressive piece of 'hey presto' that Don Hunt would have been proud of, they then claim these 'lost and found' animals as a "real" increase in the population. The statistics and terminology used by Marwell and others in this 'Great Grevy's Zebra Rally' are woefully inadequate, amateurish and, quite frankly, bordering on the burlesque, and as such, practically negate the supposed purpose behind the census. This elusive herd of animals was composed of some 300 very tangible, adult zebras, which had somehow been missed in the previous 2016 census. If one examines the statistics supplied by Marwell, one could easily extrapolate all manner of unreasonable figures and estimates from the two censuses. For instance, in the 2016 survey, they claim a population of 2,350 animals – plus or minus 93 zebra – and in the 2018 census they quote a population of 2,812 animals – plus or minus 163. So, by adding the 300 'missing' zebras to the 2016 census, and then taking into account the enormous sample variability factors, this so-called "real increase in the population" is negligible.

Obviously, the major errors in these population surveys from 2016 and 2018 are; firstly the 'lost and found' 300 Grevy's zebra which represent a significant 12% of the entire Kenyan population, and secondly the extraordinarily high 'plus and minus' figures that are given in the census. In this case, we have a 'plus and minus' value '163' in the 2018 census, which represents 6% of the total Grevy's population.

The golden rule with statistics like this, that employ 'plus and minus' values, is that the higher your 'plus-minus' variability the less precise is your estimate. In other words, these censuses and surveys are of almost no value whatsoever.

The problem here, is that these types of population surveys of East African ungulates are notoriously unreliable, just as in 2008 and 2010 when aerial surveys of the Grevy's zebra population did not extend into the Grevy's northern range because of the prohibitive costs involved. As we can see, the recent ground surveys appear to be just as flawed, making it almost impossible to peer into this morass and come up with any reasonable estimate of the present status of the endangered Grevy's zebra. Especially when we take into consideration that this 'Great Grevy's Zebra Rally', a census, only includes 5 Kenyan counties out of a total of 47, which is akin to estimating the population of the entire United Kingdom by counting how many people live in five different parishes in Hampshire.

However, what we can say with some degree of confidence is that the Grevy's zebra population has not seen a substantial or a sustainable increase since Marwell Zoo and most of those other organisations became involved in the 'conservation' of that animal in the late '70s.

Some quotes from the official report on the present status of the Grevy's zebra reveals a discrepancy between the glop of Marwell's report and the real situation. Statements like: "numbers seem to be slightly higher in 2018 than in 2016." do not inspire a great deal of confidence in what these 'conservation' organisations, like Marwell, are actually doing down there in Kenya. That particular statement is almost ludicrous, and is taking ambiguity to a new level, for how can 'numbers **seem** to be **slightly** higher'?

One is reminded of Marwell's statement concerning the Scimitar-Horned oryx in Tunisia; that they had "found **almost** no dead adult oryx."

Another comment on the 2018 census: "increases are not statistically significant" directly contradicts the claim of a "very real increase" in the population.

This is confirmed by a further statement that "reduced overall fecundity" - a decrease of what they call new "recruits"; foals - from 30% in 2016 to 22% in 2018, leads to the fairly damning conclusion that:

"Only in Laikipia county did the proportion of 'recruits' approach levels that could maintain population sustainability" and "Overall the counties with the largest populations showed no statistically significant change."

Laikipia is one of the smallest counties in Kenya, at a mere 8,690 sq. km. - whilst counties like Samburu, Isiolo and Tana River are all well over 20,000 sq. km. - meaning that it was only in one of the smallest and most localised populations in Kenya that enough foals had been produced to "approach levels that could maintain population sustainability".

So does this mean that the Grevy's Zebra population was shown to be unsustainable throughout all 47 counties of Kenya, and only "approaching" sustainability in that one small county of Laikipia?

All of which appears to make the claim of an "increase" in the Grevy's population in 2018 somewhat incomprehensible. It actually shows that the imperilled situation of the Imperial remains largely untouched by this plethora of zoos and other organisations who jump on the bandwagon to trumpet their own conservation "success" story with the species.

Serious doubts must be raised about any positive or up-beat reports from Marwell - or any other organisation - concerning an alleged increase in the Grevy's zebra population from 2016 to 2018, as it must be remembered that in 2017 the areas of Kenya most densely populated by Grevy's zebra were hit by one of the most devastating droughts in living memory, causing the greatest number of mortalities amongst them since population fluctuations began to be recorded in the early 2000s.

Estimates are not particularly easy to find or access but it appears that at least 5% of the Grevy's zebra population was wiped out, with reports of up to 120 animals dying in one restricted area alone. A situation that would have been much worse if it had not been for the noble efforts of the Grevy's Zebra Trust and others to supplement their feed by putting out 3,500 bales of hay for them and providing much needed water resources.

Meanwhile, far away from the glare and glitter of their photo-shoots and fancy-dress launch parties for yet more glossy brochures of how they saved the Grevy's zebra from extinction, there are very real people taking very real steps to do something other than count and take photos of them, to radically improve the precarious and parlous situation of the Grevy's zebra in Kenya. They are native Kenyans with no connection whatsoever to Marwell or any other zoo, who are being assisted quietly and without fanfare by the Grevy's Zebra Trust in a, for once, genuine attempt to save this endangered species from extinction. Their approach is to address the real issues behind the demise of the Imperial, rather than using the threat of domestic livestock encroachment and 'poaching' to raise funds, as many organisations - particularly zoos like Marwell – continue to do.

It is not invasive domestic livestock that represent the greatest threat to the Grevy's zebra, but rather the lack of any kind of practical land management, particularly livestock rotation, on the grazing lands occupied by both the pastoralist tribal livestock owners and the Grevy's zebra. This lack has been very much the case in the past, but now co-operative ventures and agreements between the pastoralist tribes and the Grevy's Zebra Trust have pioneered a livestock management system - introduced by ecologist Allan Savory - which also caters for wild grazers, as well as providing much-needed relief to the local communities during severe droughts, as in 2017 and 2019. Domestic livestock actually fertilize and prepare the future fodder for the wild grazers like the Grevy's zebra, just as long as the herds are moved on, according to an agreed rotation, before the grazing land is completely depleted. One observer noted about this totally unique system that it had been "the **decisive** factor behind the Grevy's zebra population stabilization after decades of decline".

So, not the 'Great Grevy's Zebra Rally' that Marwell lays claims to then, or the counting, or the photo snaps of zebras, that has stabilized the population, but rather a simple piece of hands-on and practical livestock husbandry.

In an earlier chapter, we saw how much of the perceived pressure on endangered animals like the Grevy's zebra was largely propaganda promoted by the very people who were the real pressure on them: the animal trappers, dealers and the zoological institutions they worked for, plus, of course, the 'Great White Hunters', who were all claiming to be trying to 'save' the animals from the "brink of extinction" at the hands of that mythical bogeyman, the 'African Poacher'. If such a mythical being ever really existed, then the small harm they caused to the wildlife of East Africa was nothing compared to the holocaust that the animal trappers, dealers, zoos like Marwell and Dvur Kralove, and the white hunters visited on these animals, while blaming the 80% decline in their numbers over the three decades that they were active, on the 'African Poacher'.

This is succinctly summed up by the 'white hunter' Martin Anderson in 1963, just after shooting dead a magnificent male Eastern Mountain bongo for a trophy, when he commented that:

"The bongo appears to be on the increase and there is not

much hunter pressure, except for the ever-present 'poacher' problem. It does seem an opportune time to try your hand for bongo... as Kerr and Downey also have been successful of late in bagging bongo."

Elsewhere in Africa, the wildlife authorities are quickly discovering that the old colonial apparatus of anti-poaching units and patrols is not fit for purpose, as it represents a total waste of effort, resources and money. For instance, in Zambia, where training and employing local villagers to act as the eyes and ears of the wildlife department - instead of highly expensive, volatile, armed anti-poaching units which divided the local communities by creating an 'us and them' situation - has resulted in a direct decrease in incidents of poaching and has, with its 'prevention is better than cure' policy, made a real contribution to the eradication of poaching.

The colonial myth of the 'gung-ho' white ranger battling against rampant gangs of local 'African' poachers though, is still alive and well, for just as Adams and McShane say in their far-sighted and portentous work from 1998, 'The Myth of Wild Africa':

"The myth that the press, conservation groups, Western governments and even African governments have built up around national parks, wildlife and Africans, is that any African in a national park, so the story goes, must be a poacher."

This is the myth which many conservationists and zoos rely on for their funding and subsequent projects in Africa. We now know that it is not and was never the case, as the vast majority of the 'poachers' were in fact Western settlers, animal dealers and trappers, who promoted this myth all over Africa to disguise their own destructive harvest of the wildlife of East Africa for themselves and for the zoological institutions that wanted to exhibit them, perversely claiming to be 'saving' those animals from extinction, plus the natural history museums and 'white' hunters who wanted trophies for their dens and collections. These were the poachers, and they still are.

Equally, it was the early efforts of the Western settlers in Kenya to raise cattle and other domestic livestock on the vast open spaces, at the enormous expense of the local communities and wildlife, which ultimately resulted in local Kenyans raising their domestic livestock on land that produced only $5 per hectare, whilst land that could support wildlife tourism, that would have provided the local Kenyans with between $50 to $100 per hectare, was mostly owned by Western settlers as private game ranches. Thus, the Grevy's Zebra Trust's initiative, in conjunction with local Kenyans, is so vital to all the inhabitants of the country's vast open spaces: the people, the livestock and the magnificent wildlife like the Grevy's zebra. Everyone wins. Whereas the only winner in Marwell's somewhat confused and addled 'conservation' strategy, is Marwell Zoo.

This idyllic vision of the local Kenyan people, their herds of domestic livestock and wild animals like the Grevy's zebra sharing the same grazing land in peaceful harmony is not an idle dream. It became a reality as long ago as 2005 when the Westgate Community Conservancy was established by the Kenyan government in Samburu county, which is now a thriving and shining example of what can be done for conservation by local Kenyans, rather than counting Grevy's in their sleep and taking photos of them. For it is here that 600 Samburu families, with their livestock, live together in perfect harmony with the largest concentration of Grevy's zebra in the world; at least 500 animals, along with many other wild species, where there is no land encroachment pressure on wild or domestic animals; and where intelligence-led security amongst the

Samburu tribe has reduced poaching to zero in the last five years. It is the slogan of the Samburu co-operative responsible for this peaceful coexistence between wildlife and humans, that demonstrates their pride in this unique experiment:

"We cherish to conserve – the Grevy's zebra is our gold."

In other words, the Grevy's zebra is proving to be a valuable resource for this tribe and they are protecting it as such. Which, when one considers that the Samburu tribe at Westgate Community Conservancy might well be responsible for perhaps as much as 90% of the entire Grevy's zebra population in Kenya, theirs is an awesome but entirely rewarding responsibility.   This is far removed from the procrastination and blunderings of Western influences, like Marwell Zoo, as they stumble across the unfamiliar landscape of East Africa in their clumsy Hampshire wellies. For just as Rowan Martin, the former deputy director of the Department of National Parks and Wildlife Management in Zimbabwe pointed out in the '90s:

"The irony is that where conservation hasn't intruded, wildlife has done very well. But people have come in with their muddled thoughts about protected species, preventing people from using wildlife and then saving it."

As the vast majority of Grevy's zebra are now in officially recognised and fully protected conservancies like the Westgate Community and the nearby Lewa Conservancy - which boasts a thriving herd of 350 animals - what, between the devil and the deep blue sea, do all these Western 'conservation' organisations like Marwell Zoo, think they are contributing by counting them, photographing them and throwing radio collars around their necks?

The local Kenyans have stepped up to the mark here, and are saving the Grevy's zebra themselves, while institutions like Marwell, have instead captive-bred their zoo stock into an early extinction. The only organisation that shines like a diamond in the rough, is the Grevy's Zebra Trust, who would do well to rid themselves of any alliance to any zoological institution, regardless of the financial benefits involved, as those zoological institutions have absolutely nothing to do with conservation, and neither should they.

Chapter Fourteen

It would be an injustice to Marwell Zoo not to recognise the fact that the zoo has been involved in a so-called 'successful' conservation exercise where there has been a crude attempt to translocate a rare species into a local habitat. However, this is not in Kenya, Tunisia, Zimbabwe or even the Kingdom of Swaziland, but rather at Farnborough Airfield in Hampshire, just up the road from Marwell Zoo, where they appear to have played a useful role in the introduction of the European sand lizard into an enclosed area of the airfield known as Eelmoor Marsh. Marwell's senior trustee admits that this local nature project, is not "in the same league" as their international role in the conservation of endangered species - one assumes the senior trustee here refers to Marwell's somewhat clumsy efforts in Kenya and Tunisia - but it is nonetheless a scheme which also allows Marwell Zoo to find a convenient home for their considerable number of surplus male Mongolian Wild horses, aka Prezwalski's horses, which have been put out to pasture along with the sand lizards at Eelmoor Marsh, which is a long way from Mongolia.

However, Mongolia is not a long way from Marwell, for it is in Mongolia that Marwell claims its 'flagship' success in the strange zoological marketplace of 'captive breeding' and 'reintroduction', due to its long-term involvement in the return of the Przewalski's horse to the wilds of Mongolia and China. This vast project involving hundreds of captive-bred animals - some of them from Marwell - has been on-going since 1985 when the first 'Takhi' - as the Przewalski is known locally in Mongolia - were released into the "semi-wild" of Xianjiang National Park in China. "Semi-wild" apparently means that the reintroduced herds are still being managed in semi-captivity, which includes being rounded up every winter and confined to enclosures, supposedly to reduce competition with the large number of domestic horses belonging to the nomadic tribes that appear to share this "semi-wilderness" with these re-introduced Takhi.

Information is, to say the least, sketchy, on the success or failure of this on-going project, but given that the first release of 27 Takhi, in 2001, totally failed with the loss of all animals, serious doubts are raised about this 'reintroduction' project. Doubts which are compounded by the fact that the 89 wild horses released in 2013 were not released at all but rather, what they call "semi-released".

Everything about these reintroductions of the Takhi seem to be semi-something, either semi-wild, semi-release or semi-captivity, but they have recently changed their terminology to call the wild horses "free-ranging", as if they are a bunch of chickens who have been thrown out of the shed and into the yard to satisfy public demands for some kind of ethics here.

A similar scheme also began in Hustai National Park in Mongolia in 1992, but yet again, there are mixed and somewhat confusing reports about the success or failure of the project, but it seems that in some years since then, there have been some very serious losses of reintroduced Przewalski's. Such as, when 17 young foals were released into the national park resulting in the death of 13 of them. Similarly, a herd of 89 Takhi released in 1992, had by 2013 - 21 years later - remained static at 89 horses, a strong indication that the population is not viable.

At the same time though, the relevant and responsible organizations and authorities involved in the project, claim that there is now a population of 500 of what they call "free-ranging" wild horses in Mongolia.

However, a recent independent survey by Japanese scientists involved in a study of the reintroduced herds of Takhi in Hustai, discovered some very serious problems with this long-term project, not the least of which was the extremely high mortality rate of the wild horses, from TBIs. In this case, resulting in deadly 'piroplasmosis', transmitted by local ticks, causing death by the now very familiar 'Theileria', albeit a different strain to that which has badly hampered the reintroduction attempts of ungulates into Africa. 'Theileria equi' is equally deadly, killing one out of every five adults in the main Takhi reserve, with 50% of all foals dying soon after birth, the net result being an average mortality rate of some 19% per year but climbing suddenly in 2015 to a worrying 29%.

We are already aware that diseases caused by TBIs usually result in a general reproductive failure, culminating in abortions and the sudden deaths of new-born foals, but this TBI, as virulent as it is, - with foals often carrying between 12 and 17 ticks - has been compounded by many of the reintroduced Takhi dying from acute 'Streptococcus equi', commonly known as 'strangles'. This disease causes extremely high mortality rates whenever the wild horses are rounded up and confined to their winter enclosures. However serious all these health threats posed to the reintroduced Takhi, the Japanese team of independent researchers did not view these as the primary threat that these animals faced, but rather, they saw the greatest threat as being the continuing hybridization of the Takhi with the domestic horses belonging to the nomad tribes who share the national park with them.

It is certainly not common knowledge that the Takhi are sharing that national park in Mongolia with over 24,000 domestic horses belonging to the 120 nomadic families also settled there. These domestic horses are the obvious source of both the deadly TBI and the equally deadly 'strangles', with which all of the domestic animals are infected but are immune to the diseases that develop as a result of infection, whilst the zoo-bred Takhi have absolutely no immunity and, as a consequence, die very quickly indeed.

The threat of hybridization between the Takhi and domestic horses is very likely as ancient as the domestication of the horse by the nomad tribes of Mongolia. Although it is a very serious issue indeed, it is usually glossed over with copious amounts of 'glop' by the somewhat embarrassed zoological world. Studies many years ago revealed that inter-breeding had been taking place between the wild and domestic horses of Mongolia since those ancient days, leaving the zoo world with what amounted to a very uncomfortable and ill-fitting 'chimera' of a crossbreed that is neither jam nor marmalade but rather a complex and unappetising chutney.

This is subject to much denial in the zoological circles concerned, as after spending over 150 years carefully breeding the Takhi to the most stringent and strictly enforced genetic profiling, in a vain attempt to 'breed out' the domestic horse from the Takhi, they are still left, over a century later, with what amounts to a hapless nag that nobody really knows what to do with. This is probably the most futile and pointless quest of the curiously blinkered modern zoo world yet, as the 13 original founder animals from which every Takhi in captivity today is descended, carried 26 alleles, 24 of these being from 'wild' Przewalski's but the other two alleles from domestic mares. Therefore, any attempt by selective breeding and genetic profiling to eliminate the domestic mare's alleles, may lead to a catastrophic loss of the 'wild' alleles as well.

This leads one to question just what the zoos of the world, and the private and government agencies that support this perilous adventure, think that they are actually achieving by introducing an expensive herd of cross-bred nags into Mongolia and China? It is utterly incomprehensible and almost beggar's belief.

Long before Marwell ever existed, in 1967, the equine specialist E. Mohr, made some very cutting and relevant remarks on the phenotype of the Przewalski's horse and his comments are as true today as they were then:

"The facts and considerations I have mentioned in this paper have shown that probably not a single Przewalski's horse living in captivity today can be considered as pure-bred. The same can be said for Przewalski's horses who eventually live still in the wilderness."

It seems from this translation that what the good professor was saying - but the zoo world chose to ignore him - is that there are no Przewalski's horses, either in the wild or captivity. It doesn't exist.

Almost fifty years later in 1990 this was followed by the, almost resigned, comments of the 'Captive Breeding Specialist Group' of the 'Species Survival Commission' of the IUCN:

"The Asian Wild Horse (Equus przewalski) is considered extinct in the wild. The Przewalski survives as a captive population and gene pool that is derived largely from Asian Wild Horse origins but contains appreciable and incompletely documented contributions from domestic horse stock. This captive population and gene pool has been subjected to variable, artificial selection over its seventy plus years in captivity. This selection has been oriented mostly towards production of a phenotype that resembles the descriptions and samples of animals from the last wild populations of the species."

Damning remarks, but at the same time very reminiscent of comments we featured in an earlier chapter about the efforts of Antwerp Zoo in the 1960's to produce a 'Bongsi', a hybrid between a bongo and a sitatunga antelope, where the Curator of Mammals at Antwerp, J. Tijskens, explained in the International Zoo Year Book that:

"The purpose of such a breeding project is to obtain an animal that at least resembles the bongo antelope."

Going back to the IUCN statement in 1990, the members of the Species Survival Commission also issued a stark warning to the zoos of the world who were still breeding Takhi willy-nilly in captivity:

"By the end of 1989, there will be 900 captive horses in the world, and we will be unable to place animals after 1992. Zoos will need to find space for surplus animals themselves; zoos should reduce breeding."

The Commission reinforced this with the comments that certain animals might be "liable for removal" from the world herd, and that their guidelines provided for "partially genetically isolated sub-populations".

Perhaps these "partially genetically isolated sub-populations" that may be "liable for removal" from the world herd were the forlorn products of the efforts of the Karl-Marx-Stadt Institute's efforts to cross breed Przelwaskis with Tarpan which had the approval for 'scientific interest' of these various commissions and committees in 1989?

The comments of the SSC of the IUCN in 1990 are what may have led to zoos all over the world, like Marwell, suddenly isolating some of their Przewalskis by removing them from the general population, perhaps as genetically 'undesirable', to be kept at what the zoos now term "outer-stations", the most famous of which is at Chernobyl, where a large herd of stray Takhis have ended up. Then, 'hey presto', along comes Eelmoor Marsh as a convenient "outer station" for Marwell's surplus, unwanted, genetically polluted, Mongolian nags and the zoo starts 'saving' sand lizards by getting them trampled under hoof by the "Przewalski's Wild Horses" as they stampede for their pony nuts of a Hampshire evening. Of course Marwell claim that the Mongolian nags are at Eelmoor Marsh as essential "grazers" to "maintain" the habitat in a manner beneficial to sand lizards, that normally only live on sand dunes and heathland.

The zoo's comments justifying this are laughable, calling the errant horses "part of a project to study their foraging habits". When it really doesn't matter what they "forage" on in a Hampshire marsh, as that won't be growing in the Hustai National Park in Mongolia. Apparently, the Mongolian animals are on an airfield in Hampshire as a "bachelor group" to provide them with an "opportunity to grow up in an appropriate social setting" - according to Marwell anyway. Surely the horses should have done that at the zoo, in the context of the herd, rather than separated off at an airfield up the road? However, that was 25 years ago in 1995, when the zoo decided to hone up the social skills of this bachelor herd, and one imagines they have long since died from the abject boredom of watching aircraft land and take-off again. That is apart from every other year when the hapless nags are painstakingly removed back to where they came from because of the International Air Show which takes place a few feet above their 'nature reserve'.

It is not far from Marwell Zoo to Farnborough Airfield, but it seems, with their project to introduce sand lizards to Eelmoor Marsh, that the zoo has set out on a very long journey indeed. As Marwell claims, in their own publicity and hype concerning this local diversion into 'conservation' in Hampshire:

"However, because sand lizards are unable to recognise suitable habitat on their own, they will continue to be dependent on conservation translocations, including reintroduction from captive breeding for the foreseeable future."

Now that statement is a licence to print banknotes and one can almost hear the feverish rasping of greedy old Don Hunt's hands, as he rubs them together in joyful glee, at hearing all that familiar and much loved glop which made him so much money for so many years... "conservation", "translocations", "captive breeding" and even "reintroduction". All in one sentence!

No matter that the sand lizards have been managing quite well for the last few million years to find "suitable habitat" without the assistance of Marwell Zoo, 'saving' them from their own tiresome inability to find a marshland sand pit in which to lay their eggs and hibernate, in a marsh.

What Marwell is saying here, is that even if they parachute 2,000 captive-bred sand lizards into Eelmoor Marsh on a daily basis, it makes no difference whatsoever to the long-term survival or expansion of the population.

It seems that they have created an unsustainable situation that is utterly dependent for its tentative and artificial equilibrium, on Marwell Zoo, to constantly "manage" the habitat and to parachute ever more captive bred sand lizards in, on a regular basis, into the "foreseeable future". So it is entirely serendipitous that they inhabit an airfield to facilitate that ongoing Berlin Airlift.

Could this be a rare admission from Marwell Zoo that 'captive-breeding' doesn't actually work?

Just in the last two years, Marwell has "reintroduced" 250 sand lizards into Eelmoor Marsh, and they plan to do this for that "foreseeable future", despite their very own PhD biology student admitting that they have only been able to account for 15% to 20% of those "reintroduced" reptiles. Rachel Gardner's comments about her field work at Eelmoor - sponsored by both Southampton University and Marwell Zoo - seem somewhat in conflict with Marwell's own ambitious efforts to spin the project out as far as they possibly can into the "foreseeable future", for she reports on the university website that:

"In total we intend for 240 individuals to be released during this reintroduction programme to **establish a self-sustaining population at the site indefinitely**."

Now that is a far cry from Marwell's stance on the Eelmoor project, with their own specialist biologist contradicting their over-played and somewhat dramatized role in relation to the 'conservation' of sand lizards. For it is not actually the fact that sand lizards "are unable to recognise suitable habitat on their own", as millions of years of evolution have given them precisely the faculty to do that very thing.

What restricts their expansion into new and suitable habitats for colonization is being confined to unsuitable habitats like Eelmoor Marsh - rather than the coastal sand dunes which are their preferred and eminently more suitable habitat.

In fact, it could well be that the original sand lizards at Eelmoor were actually the result of one of the many private attempts at reintroduction of this species, that appear to have been taking place in the United Kingdom for many years.

Whatever the case, at Eelmoor Marsh, sand lizards are subject to human interference through agriculture, forestry, drainage works or other man-made influences - such as living on an airfield which hosts one of the biggest International Air Shows in the world, where they are unable to expand either their range or population due to the artificial restrictions of their immediate environment.

This particular problem was solved many years ago by various private individuals and organisations committed to the preservation of the habitat of the sand lizard, who constructed what they called "connectivity corridors" which allowed the sand lizards to easily and freely expand their range from one location to another in order to successfully colonize habitat patches of approximately 5 hectares as a "viable population at that site indefinitely". These simple measures radically reduce the risk of local extinction. Again, a direct contradiction to Marwell's stated manifesto and thereby negating their claim to "need" to put thousands of sand lizards into a swamp with no sand. A swamp which was called Eelmoor Marsh because it was a 'marsh' that eels liked but not suitable habitat for 'sand' lizards or even Przewalski's horses for that matter.

If Marwell's errant herd of Asian Wild Horses are kept at Eelmoor as grazers to ensure that the habitat is "managed" and maintained at the optimal level for the conservation of the sand lizards, then why did they bring in heavy earth-moving machinery to remove dense vegetation from the site in 2017, when earlier, the zoo had claimed that the horses were at Eelmoor to keep "aggressive vegetation in check"?

Recent studies have shown beyond a doubt, that the use of heavy earth-moving machinery in such an environmentally sensitive area - which Eelmoor Marsh is - would have been extremely detrimental to the sand lizards, especially when they are hibernating in December, which is exactly when Marwell chose to undertake such a dangerous escapade. These same studies also revealed that over-extensive management of the habitat of small and isolated populations of sand lizards could lead to rapid extirpation in that area. The herpetologist, C.W. Painter commented in 2004 that:

"Virtually nothing is known about the potential direct impact of livestock grazing on sand lizards and its habitat"

Meanwhile, some 200 or so Scimitar-Horned oryx stare out from their fenced enclosures in Tunisia, at the wastelands of oblivion, right out across the Saharan desert to Chad, from where their ancestors unwillingly came, some fifty years ago, when the zoos of the world, like Marwell, practically wiped them out with their insatiable greed to have those highly endangered animals as exhibits in their vain-glorious menageries. For it is in Chad that some 250 reintroduced Scimitar-Horned oryx, in the remote and magnificent wilderness of the 'Ouadi Rime-Ouadi Achim' nature reserve, stare back across that desert at those refugee oryx in Tunisia.

Marwell recently announced that:

"The breeding of oryx in captivity has enabled the reintroduction of Scimitar-Horned oryx into Chad, where the oryx are now beginning to breed in the wild, and to reintroductions to protected areas of Tunisia."

Well, that is mostly glop.

Marwell is careful not to point out that it is not the 156 zoos involved who have bred the Chad oryx in captivity, because with an impoverished population growth of a mere 9.5% over the last few decades, those 156 zoos are not in a position to contribute oryx in any meaningful number to the proposed establishment of a population of some 500 to 1000 animals in Chad.

Rather, it has been the open, honest and transparent efforts of a few Texan ranchers and the benevolent rulers of a Gulf State, who have increased that animal's population in captivity by a massive 400% in just a few years, thus enabling them to undertake the mammoth task of sending hundreds of their captive bred oryx back to the very same Chad, where zoos like Marwell paid trappers to take out most of the last remaining Scimitar-Horned oryx back in the '60s.

There is some kind of poetic justice at work here, as the oryx are being released back into the wilds of Chad - some 250 oryx to date - in exactly the same place that the animal dealer Van den Brink, captured the very last herd of wild Scimitar-Horned oryx at the behest of Marwell Zoo and others: the Ouadi Rime-Ouadi Achim.

Obviously, those same zoological institutions that are indirectly responsible for the eventual extinction of the

Scimitar in the wild, are now attaching themselves like so many remora to the underbelly of the magnificent behemoth that has suddenly loomed into their ocean, to return the Scimitars finally, back into the wilds of Chad, from where those zoos removed them, over fifty years ago.

Given Marwell's resounding failure to reintroduce the Scimitar-Horned oryx back into the wilds of Tunisia, and elsewhere, we can but marvel that a representative of Marwell Zoo gave a talk to the 'Technical Workshop' which gathered to discuss the Chad project in 2012, on the 'success' of Marwell's Tunisian reintroduction of Scimitars. This was followed by a report that the zoo submitted to the Chad project in 2018, entitled: "Antelope Conservation: Exporting Experience from Tunisia across the Sahara."

When read with the zoo's latest comment on the sad Tunisian oryx affair stating that:

"We now focus on factors that will affect the long-term health of these populations."

One could suggest to Marwell Zoo, to perhaps focus on "exporting" their refugee Scimitar-Horned oryx - currently stranded in Tunisia - to Chad, rather than their "experience".

Volume II of 'Tainted Blood' is in the process of assimilation.

Lightning Source UK Ltd.
Milton Keynes UK
UKHW011832310820
369128UK00001B/29

9 781839 454189